THE STORY OF CANADA

JANET LUNN • CHRISTOPHER MOORE
Illustrated by ALAN DANIEL

SCHOLASTIC CANADA LTD.
New York Toronto London Auckland Sydney
Mexico City New Delhi Hong Kong Buenos Aires

For Elizabeth, Liam, Kieran, and Joe
– born during the writing of *The Story of Canada*

Scholastic Canada Ltd.
604 King Street West, Toronto, Ontario M5V 1E1, Canada

Scholastic Inc.
557 Broadway, New York, NY 10012, USA

Scholastic Australia Pty Limited
PO Box 579, Gosford, NSW 2250, Australia

Scholastic New Zealand Limited
Private Bag 94407, Greenmount, Auckland, New Zealand

Scholastic Children's Books
Euston House, 24 Eversholt Street, London NW1 1DB, UK

Library and Archives Canada Cataloguing in Publication

Lunn, Janet, 1928-
The story of Canada : the making of a nation / Janet
Lunn, Christopher Moore ; illustrated by Alan Daniel.
Previously published as part of : The story of
Canada. Toronto : Key Porter Books, 2007.
Includes bibliographical references and index.
ISBN 978-0-545-99617-4
1. Canada--History--1763-1867--Juvenile literature.
2. Canada--History--Confederation, 1867--Juvenile literature.
3. Canada--Biography--Juvenile literature.
I. Moore, Christopher, 1950- II. Daniel, Alan, 1939- III. Title.
FC172.L852 2009 j971.05 C2009-904112-X

Published in arrangement with Key Porter Books Limited
This edition published by Scholastic Canada Ltd. in 2009

Care has been taken to trace ownership of copyright material contained in this book. The publishers will gladly receive any information that will enable them to rectify any reference or credit line in subsequent editions.
See pp. 114 for full picture credits.

6 5 4 3 2 1 Printed in Canada 09 10 11 12 13

Opposite: The Young Reader. NGC/© Ozias Leduc 1992/VIS*ART.

To the Reader

We have called this book
The Story of Canada,
but we know no book has
room for all the stories of
Canada. We hope you find
something of yourself in the
tales we have told – and go
on to discover more stories
of Canada for yourself.

The Authors

Contents

Chapter 1

The Great Northwest

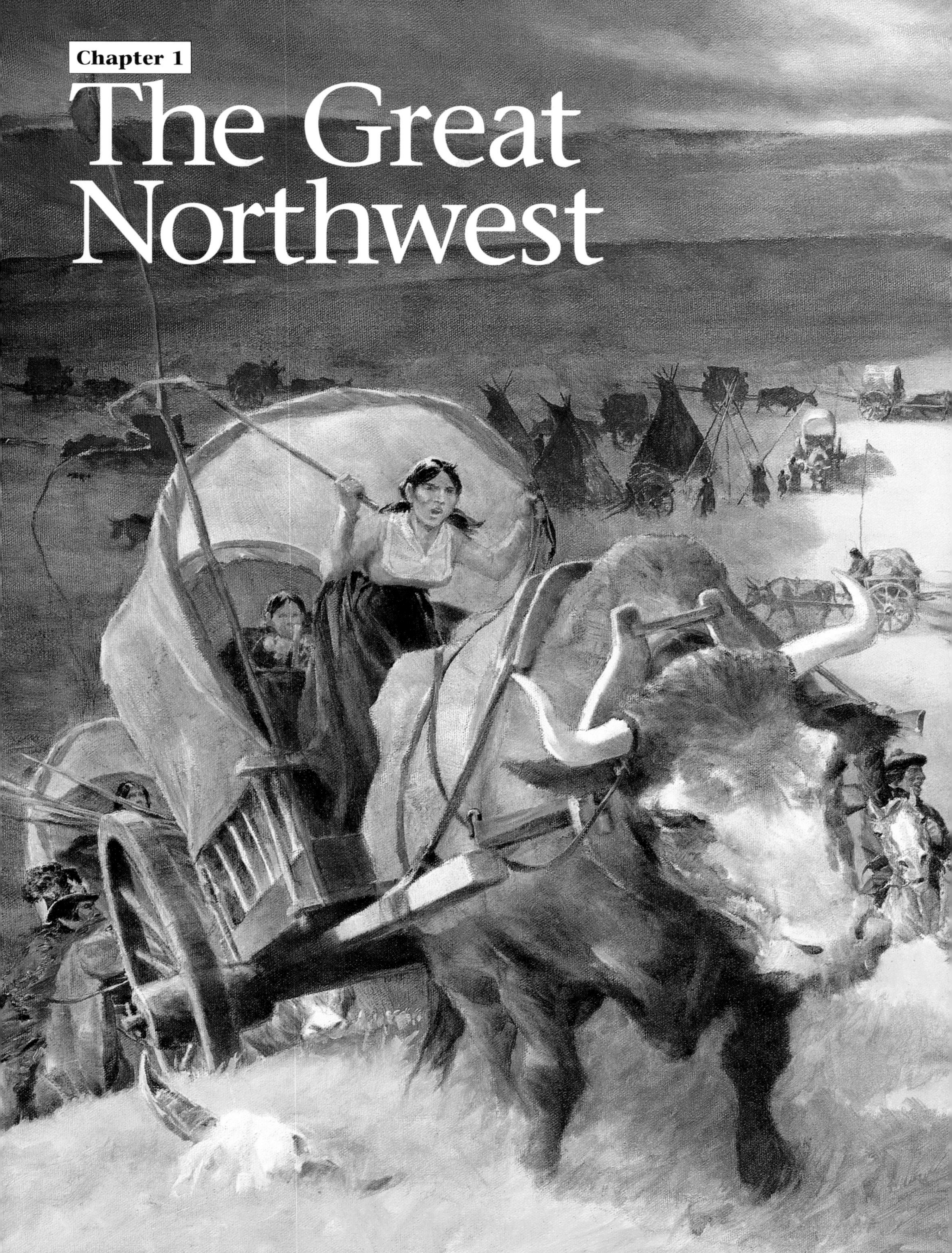

FIVE HUNDRED YEARS AGO, 60 MILLION BISON – OR BUFFALO, AS they are more often called – roamed the grasslands of North America. They meant life itself to plains nations like the Blackfoot of what is now southern Alberta. The Blackfoot moved slowly across the land, following the herds and carrying with them everything they had. They hunted deer and antelope, they grew tobacco, and they gathered wild turnip and onion. But for centuries it was the buffalo that provided for the Blackfoot people. Buffalo hides made their tipis and their clothing. Buffalo sinews were their thread. Buffalo bones made clubs and spoons and needles. They even used dried buffalo dung as fuel for their campfires. To the Blackfoot, buffalo meat was "real" meat and nothing else tasted so good. They trusted the buffalo to keep them strong.

The Blackfoot had always gone on foot, using dogs to help carry their goods, for there were no horses in North America until Spanish colonists brought them in the 1500s. Soon after that, plains people captured animals that had gone wild, or stole them in raids. They traded the horses northward and, early in the 1700s, horses came to the northern plains. Suddenly the Blackfoot were a nation on horseback. How exciting it was, learning to ride a half-wild mustang and galloping off to the horizon!

Soon everyone on the plains could ride. Horses carried people and their belongings as they roved the plains. Horses became the proudest possessions of the Blackfoot and their neighbours. Hunters and warriors virtually lived on horseback. Now, instead of waiting for the buffalo, young men rode full gallop, bow in hand, into stampeding herds. To pick out and kill one's prey took magnificent horsemanship and cool courage.

Young men gloried in the excitement of it. They gloried in war, too, although war was even more dangerous and exciting on horseback than it had been before. The plains nations had always celebrated pride and courage, and young men had always sought to outdo each other in feats of bravery. Above all, they competed for *coups.* A coup meant coming close enough to touch an enemy,

Previous page
Métis cart brigades ranged the Prairies in search of buffalo herds. These families are starting the long trail back to Red River, their carts packed with pemmican after a successful hunt.

Head-Smashed-In Buffalo Jump

A "buffalo jump," like that shown here, was sometimes used in the buffalo hunt. One well-known site is Head-Smashed-In Buffalo Jump, which stands in the Porcupine Hills above the Oldman River in southern Alberta. From the top of the cliff, the plain seems to flow eastward forever. That view was the last thing ever seen by thousands and thousands of buffalo.

Archeologists say Head-Smashed-In Buffalo Jump was used by Native Canadians for more than five thousand years. In the mounds of earth at the foot of the cliffs, buffalo bones piled up ten metres deep. There people came to harvest food and to thank the spirit of the buffalo for its gift.

Today, Head-Smashed-In Buffalo Jump is a World Heritage Site. A museum stands close by the cliff's edge. Members of the Blackfoot Confederacy explain the lore of the buffalo to visitors. At the top of the cliff, in the constant wind, it is easy to feel that the spirit of the buffalo still lives.

and it was worth risking death for such glory. The bravest warriors, with many coups and many eagle feathers in their magnificent war bonnets, became honoured leaders of their people.

The Blackfoot were not beaver trappers, for there were no beaver on the plains. North of the Blackfoot and the buffalo, however, shimmering aspen forests lined the valley of the North Saskatchewan River. Still farther north, in a land dotted with lakes, stretched the dark spruce forest. This was fine country for beaver. Since Samuel de Champlain's day, beaver had meant fur traders. Peoples of the woodlands took eagerly to the fur trade. Some became hunters and trappers, while others became traders.

The Buffalo Hunt, Four Hundred Years Ago

At dawn, on a clear fall day, the Blackfoot people prayed to the spirit of the buffalo. If you had been there, you would have been shivering even in your warm deerskin shirt or shift and leggings.

Imagine you are there . . . .

Two days ago the scouts went out. Last night they came back to report that the herd was near. The best poundmakers in the band have done their work. They have chosen the strongest willow stakes and driven them into the hard ground to form the V-shaped fence of the jumping pound. At the narrow end of the pound is a small opening, right at the edge of the cliff.

Your feet in their moccasins are cold as you creep through the tall, frost-tipped grass. You have learned to read the land so well that you know the signs of prairie-dog holes, ant hills, and gullies. You go silently, as though you knew every stalk of grass.

You hear the geese honking overhead, the killdeer's shrill cry nearby. The scent of sagebrush is in your nostrils. Then you sniff buffalo.

The buffalo are coming!

Out behind the herd, three young men have wrapped themselves in grey wolf pelts. They move towards the herd, and the wolf smell makes the buffalo move away, bellowing nervously. The herd begins to flow towards you. You can feel the earth drumming under the thunder of their hoofs.

You are lying in the tall, cold grass with the women and the other children, forming two lines like beads on two strings. The beasts draw near, and one by one you stand. The buffalo move between the lines. How hot and stinking they are! The next person stands, and the next. Now it's your turn. You stand. Everyone is up. You all walk forward, closing in on the herd. Behind the herd, hunters flap pelts and fire arrows. Terror is in the buffalo, in the people, in the air itself, as the herd sweeps into the pound. Will the wooden stakes hold?

The stakes do hold and the herd is jammed together. Surging ahead, the herd drives its leaders through the opening at the narrow end of the pound. Over the cliff they go to their deaths, and the rest follow.

Now the skinning and butchering begin. Shoving frantic, barking dogs from underfoot, you work all day with your stone knives. You can feel the eyes of the hungry coyotes watching from the edge of the pound. Tonight there will be a feast. Every tipi will have a pot full of meat and wild onion. There will be singing and dancing to the music of the drum and the eagle-bone flute. There will be dice-playing and storytelling. And you will honour the spirit of the buffalo, who gave you this herd. This meat and hide and sinew and bone will keep your people strong. There will be food in the winter camp, down in a sheltered valley with a stream and a grove of trees. This year, all but the oldest and most feeble will live through to spring.

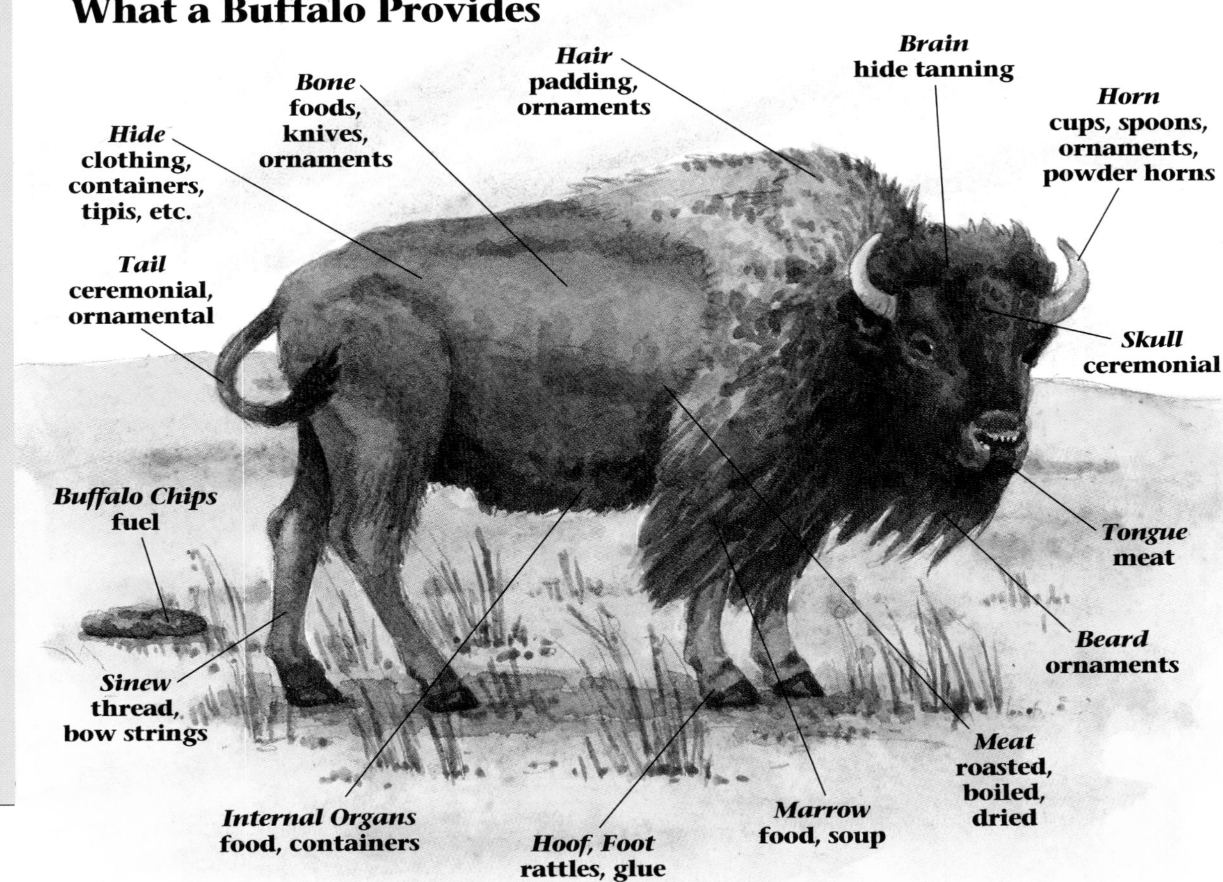

Many keen traders came from the Cree nation. The Cree homeland lay in the woods, close to the trading posts on Hudson Bay, but Cree traders travelled west along the Saskatchewan River with the goods they bartered from the Baymen. Some of the traders settled along the river, and soon they were trading with the Blackfoot of the plains. The Blackfoot had horses while the Cree had muskets, and exchanging guns and horses sealed their friendship. They rode together to fight old enemies, the Sioux and the Snakes. Some of the Cree put aside their trade canoes and took to the grasslands, riding horses and hunting buffalo as the other plains people did.

The Fur Traders' Rivalry

From London, the "Company of Adventurers Trading into Hudson's Bay" sent its sailing ships through northern seas to its lonely trading posts on Hudson Bay. The most imposing was Prince of Wales's Fort, whose thick stone walls and heavy cannon guarded the mouth of the Churchill River. Few of the Hudson's Bay Company traders who manned it, and other posts like it, ever ventured farther into the country. Cree, Ojibwa, and Chipewyan traders, travelling along mysterious rivers from the heart of the continent, brought the furs to the company's trading posts by the bay.

The fur traders of Montreal did not wait for others to bring beaver pelts to them. Since the days of Radisson and Groseilliers, Montreal's adventurers had carried their trade

The rivers and lakes of Canada were highways of travel and trade for thousands of years. Every route included many portages, where canoes and goods had to be carried overland on straining shoulders.

Explorer Alexander Mackenzie argues about the geography of the western rivers with tough trader Peter Pond. Alexander's cousin, the scholarly Roderick Mackenzie, who was the North West Company's factor at Fort Chipewyan, listens intently. Pond's advice sent Alexander, who was searching for the Pacific, down the Mackenzie River – to the Arctic Ocean instead.

goods up the rivers of the pays d'en haut in birchbark canoes. They wintered in the distant Northwest, always searching for new nations to trade with. With the help of their Native trading partners, they carried the fur trade almost to the Rocky Mountains. Each year, canoe brigades returned triumphantly to Montreal with bales of beaver pelts. Montreal and Hudson Bay competed for the fur trade of half a continent.

After Britain conquered New France, young Scots immigrants came to Montreal to join in the fur-trading business of the French-Canadian adventurers, and they competed with the Hudson's Bay Company as fiercely as the French merchants had. Voyageurs from farms along the St. Lawrence still paddled the trade canoes from Montreal, but they were joined now by Scots and Iroquois settled along the great river. They pushed farther west, rebuilding forts on the western plains where La Vérendrye had explored, and they scooped furs from right under the noses of the Baymen.

In the 1780s, the Scots traders of Montreal got together to create the North West Company – the Nor'Westers – one united team against the Hudson's Bay Company empire. Now began the glory days of Montreal's fur trade. The Montrealers manned trading posts on distant rivers far west of Hudson Bay. They intercepted Native traders before they

Journey to the Coppermine

Samuel Hearne was a happy young man when the governor of the Hudson's Bay Company's Prince of Wales's Fort chose him to head an expedition to the Coppermine River. He was to search for the Northwest Passage and discover whether there really was copper at the mouth of the Coppermine.

The governor chose Hearne's guides, and he chose badly. The guides deserted near the remote Dubawnt River country in "the land of little sticks." There the party got lost, and the wind tore Hearne's compass from his hands and it broke on the ground. The guides stole everything else and deserted.

Hearne was alone in the frozen barrens without food or shelter. He began to walk, just to keep himself awake, but finally he collapsed.

Then, suddenly, a tall, imposing figure appeared. It was Matonabbee, a man Hearne knew well – a respected leader of the Chipewyans. Matonabbee knew the guides had deserted, and he had been out looking for Hearne. He had brought food and otter robes, and when Hearne was warm and fed, the two set out. They reached the Prince of Wales's Fort in two months, stayed for just twelve days, then left again for the Coppermine River.

They reached the Coppermine to discover that there was exactly one lump of copper to be found. But the trip was not a failure. In the two years it took, from 1770 to 1772, Hearne learned to survive by dressing as the Natives did and eating what they ate. And perhaps the greatest good to come from the trip for both Hearne and Matonabbee was the friendship that lasted all their lives.

could reach Hudson Bay, and bargained for all the furs they could get. The partners of the North West Company became merchant princes. From the magnificent Beaver Club in Montreal, they ruled a trading empire that reached out across the continent.

Nor'Westers kept pushing into new territory, and Peter Pond led the way. Pond was a violent man whose rivals always seemed to die in mysterious circumstances, and no one pushed voyageurs harder than he did. Hauling their canoes and goods over long portages, Pond's men reached Lake Athabasca in Saskatchewan's far north in 1778. From there, rivers led north and west into rich beaver country. Earlier explorers had searched for a land of gold called Eldorado. Now Athabasca country, with its cold northern rivers and thousands of beaver ponds, became the fur traders' Eldorado.

Blanket coats, knives, muskets – and whisky – were familiar items of the fur trade for hundreds of years. The ones shown here were Hudson's Bay Company trade goods around 1870.

From Montreal to the Athabasca country the canoe route stretched 7000 kilometres, and the Nor'Westers needed a "halfway house." In 1804 they built Fort William where the city of Thunder Bay now stands. Nor'Wester sailing ships carried trade goods through the Great Lakes to Fort William. From there, voyageurs in their canoes took the goods west and brought back the furs. Every June these "winterers" met their Montreal partners at Fort William for a month of wild celebration – and for hard-headed planning, too.

Shrewd planning was certainly needed. By 1800, the Nor'Westers and the Baymen were at each other's throats. Hudson's Bay traders no longer waited by their "frozen sea" while the Nor'Westers scooped up all the trade. The Baymen had moved inland to challenge their Montreal rivals, and soon their York boats were plying the rivers from Hudson Bay into the beaver country. Hudson's Bay Company forts began to dot the Northwest, starting with Cumberland House in Saskatchewan in 1774.

The Nor'Westers fought to keep the Baymen out. Nor'Westers undercut Bay prices for trade goods, and paid whatever they had to for furs. They destroyed Bay forts and canoes. They challenged inexperienced Baymen to fights and duels. They tried to starve them out. They even committed murder, sure that in that wild country no one was likely to be caught or convicted. Rival traders spent long winters thousands of kilometres from home, glaring at each other and hurling insults from tiny trading houses only a hundred metres apart. From the 1780s to 1821, a fur war raged across the West, touching many people besides the traders themselves.

The People in Between

In April 1806, Marie-Anne Gaboury married Jean-Baptiste Lagimodière in their village near Trois-Rivières on the St. Lawrence. Until then, Marie-Anne had lived a quiet life as the parish priest's housekeeper. Jean-Baptiste had just come back from five years in the pays d'en haut.

Lagimodière was a restless man, not suited to farming. He told his bride he was going west with the fur brigades. "*Bien*," she said. "If you won't stay here, I'll go with you." Friends and neighbours said she was mad. But on a warm May day, Marie-Anne set off with her new husband for the fur traders' rendezvous at Lachine, where Jean-Baptiste signed on with the North West Company as a voyageur.

The voyageurs waved their caps in the air. Then, with a flashing of paddles, four canoes loaded to the gunwales with trade goods surged into the river. In big *canots du maître* and smaller *canots du nord*, the voyageurs were on their way to the distant beaver country around Lake Athabasca. Jean-Baptiste and Marie-Anne were not going quite so far, but it would be late summer before they reached Fort Garry, where Winnipeg now stands.

Once they were out west, Jean-Baptiste and Marie-Anne travelled the rivers by canoe and followed buffalo trails in oxcarts. In the woods they trapped beaver and traded for pelts. On the plains they hunted buffalo for the voyageurs. They wintered at forts as far apart as Fort Garry and Fort Edmonton.

Marie-Anne Lagimodière came to know the aspen

Fort Garry, at the forks of the Red and Assiniboine rivers, was the centre of the Hudson's Bay Company's fur trade at Red River. Later, the company built Lower Fort Garry, 30 kilometres away. Lower Fort Garry still stands, but it was the fort at the forks of the rivers that grew into the city of Winnipeg.

groves of the broad valley of the North Saskatchewan River and the dark forests and beaver meadows farther north. She also knew the rolling drylands of the buffalo and the buffalo hunters, where the tall prairie grass stretched away as far as the eye could see, rippling in the wind. She would spend the rest of her life in the West – and she would live to be ninety-five.

By 1810 the Lagimodières had several children, and they decided to settle along the Red River. They went to live among the French-speaking Métis people there. Métis means "mixed" in French, and the Métis were so called because they had emerged from the mixing of Europeans and Native people. At Detroit or Sault Ste. Marie on the Great Lakes, by Lake Nipigon in the north woods, or along the Churchill River near Hudson Bay, every woodland trading post became a little community. French and English traders and voyageurs married Ojibwa or Cree women. Their children and grandchildren, half Native and half European, grew up and found work around the forts. They became "the people in between," the ones who knew both Natives and newcomers. They worked with both, and soon the fur trade could not get along without them. At first many of "the people in between" were French and Ojibwa. Later many were Scots and Cree. Whoever their ancestors were, they became a new and separate people, the Métis.

The Métis moved west with the fur trade. While the Nor'Westers and the Baymen fought, Métis families moved out onto the plains. They took to horses and buffalo hunting and became as skilled as the plains people. Buffalo meat, pounded, mixed with fat and berries, and packed into a hide bag, made a food called pemmican. Pemmican was a light and compact load in voyageur canoes, and the paddlers took long journeys on a diet of little else. As the war of Nor'Westers and Baymen raged on, both sides needed pemmican – particularly the Nor'Westers, whose voyageurs made the longest journeys.

By the early 1800s, the heart of the Métis country lay in the valleys of the Red and Assiniboine rivers, flowing down to Lake Winnipeg. And so, when they settled at Red River in 1810, the Lagimodières linked their future with that of the Métis.

Soon after the Lagimodières arrived, other pioneers came from overseas to settle at Red River. An eccentric Scottish aristocrat, the Earl of Selkirk, decided to make Red River into a colony for poor immigrants from the Scottish

This painting, Red River Settler's House and Cart, *was done by William Hind in 1870.*

highlands. Selkirk had bought control of the Hudson's Bay Company by then, so it granted him a territory of 300000 square kilometres: Assiniboia, on the banks of the Red River. Selkirk wanted his highlanders to grow crops and raise animals. In the midst of the fur trade country, he expected them to build a little British colony.

The Red River War

Hudson's Bay Company ships dropped the first of Selkirk's settlers at Churchill in the fall of 1811, the worst possible time of the year. They struggled overland to Red River – and starvation. Only help from the Métis and from Chief Peguis of the nearby Saulteaux people saved them. Peguis's people led the settlers south, with the children riding on Saulteaux ponies, until they reached the Métis buffalo hunters. Jean-Baptiste and Marie-Anne Lagimodière advised and helped them too. More of Selkirk's settlers arrived the next year, and things were just as hard for them.

Lord Selkirk, with some of his settlers, is shown naming Kildonan in 1817. The settlers had survived many hardships since their arrival at Churchill in 1811.

Though Métis families helped the bedraggled newcomers, they feared Lord Selkirk's plans. So did the Nor'Westers. Selkirk's colony took land that the Métis considered their own, and, as well, it lay on the route of the North West Company voyageurs. Nor'Westers feared that the Selkirk settlement was a Hudson's Bay Company plot to block their canoe brigades from reaching the Athabasca country, or to deny them the pemmican they bought from Métis hunters.

Selkirk's colony seemed doomed to disaster. Food was scarce when their first crops failed. The settlers feared the Métis and the voyageurs, and they hated the harsh winters. The Nor'Westers played on these fears. In 1815 they urged the highlanders to abandon Red River and head for Upper Canada in company canoes. The Selkirk colonists hesitated. They set out, but then they turned back. They had decided to stay and fight for Red River.

On the afternoon of June 19, 1816, a band of Métis

horsemen rode past Fort Douglas, the Hudson's Bay post used by Lord Selkirk's governor, Robert Semple. Semple rode out with twenty-six men to challenge the Métis. The two parties met at a place called Seven Oaks. Both sides were armed, and both sides were angry. Semple wanted the Métis to accept the authority Lord Selkirk had given him. The Métis were furious at being ordered about by this intruder on their land. The two sides quarrelled and shots rang out. Semple and his men were no match for the Métis hunters. In a few minutes, the governor and twenty of his men lay dead. That night the Métis, who had lost only one man, sat inside Fort Douglas, chanting songs about their victory at Seven Oaks.

Lord Selkirk was far away in Montreal, but he fought back. The Baymen at Fort Douglas had already sent Jean-Baptiste Lagimodière east to warn Selkirk of the trouble brewing, and Selkirk rushed west, bringing soldiers to defend his settlers. At Fort William he arrested the partners of the North West Company, since he blamed Montreal fur traders for the killings. Then he marched on to Red River to take charge there.

Métis leader Cuthbert Grant's mild, round face does not look like that of a brilliant horseman and guerrilla fighter. But the Red River settlers discovered his fearsome skills at Seven Oaks in 1816, when his Métis hunters killed twenty of the pioneers.

Happily for Red River, there were no more massacres. Over the next few seasons, the settlers and the Métis were too busy battling locusts and floods to fight each other. And the fur trade war was finally ending. It had been ruining both companies. The Nor'Westers had more furs, more men, and more forts, but the Hudson's Bay Company had more money. In 1821 the Hudson's Bay Company bought the North West Company and hired its best men. Montreal's fur trade died away. After two hundred years, voyageurs no longer left Lachine on the long route to the pays d'en haut. Now all the furs went out through Hudson Bay.

The Bay's Empire

The Hudson's Bay Company was a century and a half old in 1821, and finally it was free of its rival from Montreal. Its trading empire stretched from Labrador to Vancouver

Island. In 1820, George Simpson had arrived from England to take charge.

Simpson was a cold, hard-hearted man but he was efficient. When he became governor of the Hudson's Bay Company and master of the fur trade, he burst upon the West like a whirlwind. He moved swiftly from post to post in a canoe paddled by specially chosen Iroquois voyageurs. After the wild times of the fur wars, George Simpson was determined that things were going to be different.

A mean, tough, determined man, George Simpson made big changes to the Hudson's Bay Company, cutting prices and closing forts. But the company began making money again.

Simpson closed down trading posts that could not pay their way. He fired traders and voyageurs. He bought only as many furs as he thought the company needed, and he paid less for them. Times grew hard for Native traders and trappers. They had always had two companies fighting over their furs, but now there was only George Simpson's company and the tough terms it offered.

Everyone in the fur trade, even those who had fought the company most fiercely, now had to work with the Baymen. Jean-Baptiste Lagimodière was content to do so, but even Cuthbert Grant, who had led the Métis riflemen at Seven Oaks, found himself working for the Bay. Without the fur traders setting them apart, the Métis and the Selkirk settlers learned to live together. The Métis had their land on one side of the Red River, the Selkirk people had theirs on the other.

Every spring, the Red River carts rolled west into buffalo country. Oxen strained at the leather harnesses, while wooden wheels rumbled and shrieked on wooden axles. Hundreds of carts crowded with hunters and their families sent clouds of dust rising over the plain. The great buffalo hunt was beginning again. The skilful Métis led the way, but now settlers from Selkirk's colony went along too. After the cart brigades found a herd, the horsemen rode into a melee of dust and noise and terrified animals. Each hunter fired across his horse's neck, then rode on, jamming another ball and more powder down the muzzle of the musket as he came up to another buffalo. The hunters competed for the most kills, but when the hunt was done everyone worked to make pemmican.

In his Assiniboine Hunting Buffalo, *artist Paul Kane captured the speed, the excitement, and the danger of the buffalo hunt.*

The spring hunt was a good time for the Métis. Men and women took pride in their riding, and the hunters boasted of their shooting, and their fearless strength. The masters of the hunt were leaders of the whole Métis nation. Before the brigades rolled back to Red River, carts piled high with pemmican bags, there was always time for a feast and a dance. Every family had its fiddler or its piper. They danced and sang inside their circle of carts, their buckskin jackets ablaze with brilliant Métis beadwork.

But trouble was looming. The plains were becoming crowded as Métis, Cree, and Ojibwa people all moved west. Since they all had horses, each prairie nation ranged over more territory. The mounted warriors of the Plains – Cree, Blackfoot, Ojibwa, Sioux, Assiniboine, and Snake – fought not just for glory, but for the buffalo that fed them all.

In the 1830s, terrible epidemics blazed across the plains. Saukamappee, a young warrior of the Plains Cree, told of riding in to attack his enemies in their tents, and finding them all dead or dying in their bedrolls. Soon after, Saukamappee's own people caught the sickness, and so did the Blackfoot. One in three died. Saukamappee never forgot those days of tears and cries of despair.

Wanderers and Artists

After the closing of Montreal's North West Company, few furs came east, but the Canadian colonies did not forget about the Northwest. Travellers and explorers who went west brought back stories of "the great lone land."

Painter Paul Kane set out from Toronto in 1845, determined to paint the West and its people. His energy impressed George Simpson, who permitted Kane to travel the Great Lakes with Hudson's Bay Company crews. Kane visited Red River and rode with the buffalo hunters. Then he pushed on across the Rockies to the Pacific, sketching and painting everywhere. When he went home and exhibited his paintings, they caused a sensation. No one back east had ever seen such images.

Other travellers, artists, and writers were also eager to explore the West. John Palliser was a cheery young Irishman who loved hunting. He wanted to dash right across the continent, hunting buffalo, grizzlies, and mountain goats as he went. But the British government decided he could do important work on the plains. Britain and the United States had agreed in 1818 that the forty-ninth parallel of latitude would be their border all the way to the Rockies. But was the land north of that line good for anything but fur trading and buffalo hunting? Fur traders, who wanted to keep out everyone else, liked to say that the West was a frozen wasteland. Americans said that a hot, dry desert stretched north to the border. If good land lay in between, the British government wanted to know. John Palliser was told to organize an expedition and find out.

Palliser's team set out from Red River in 1857. For three years his scientists studied the country. Palliser shot buffalo to keep them fed, but he had to be a diplomat as well. The land still belonged to the Cree and Blackfoot, and Palliser's men sometimes met their war parties ranging the plains on their mustangs.

Palliser told Britain's government of a huge territory too dry for farming, too dry for settlers. This triangular area in what is now southern Saskatchewan and Alberta became

A young Irishman who loved hunting, shooting, and fishing, John Palliser just wanted adventure on the Canadian plains. But in 1856 the British government gave him a bigger job. It needed to know if those distant plains were fit for farming and for settlement. Yes, said Palliser, after three years travelling the West – but not the dry part, called Palliser's Triangle.

William Hind, Bar in a Mining Camp. *In 1862, William Hind set off with the Overlanders on their arduous voyage to the Cariboo goldfields of British Columbia. The Overlanders must often have felt as weary as these men at a mining camp appear to be.*

known as Palliser's Triangle. Palliser also told of a rich "fertile belt" farther north. This was no frozen wasteland. It had fine agricultural prospects.

Interest in the West continued to grow, and not only in Britain. In Canada West, where farmland was becoming scarce, farmers who wondered where their children would find land began looking west. George Brown, a young newspaperman from Toronto, began to preach in *The Globe* that Canada must colonize and settle the West. The way Canadians talked, it was as though the entire prairie was an empty land waiting for them to come west with their ploughs.

Leaders of the West

Red River people knew the land was not empty. Marie-Anne and Jean-Baptiste Lagimodière's children and grandchildren had grown up at Red River among the Métis people. The Métis were now mainly farmers and traders, but many of their hunters had moved farther west to settle along the rivers of Saskatchewan and Alberta. They still sold pemmican to the Baymen, but they would not let George Simpson's company push them around. The Bay claimed that it controlled the fur trade of all the West, but in 1849 a Métis trader sold his furs to an American trading

Previous pages:
Geese wing northward as the boat builders of Fort Edmonton put the finishing touches to a new York boat. Looking on is Chief Factor John Rowand, the big, friendly, and energetic fur trader who ran Fort Edmonton for thirty years.

post across the border. Although the company took him to a Red River court, he walked out unpunished. Led by Marie-Anne's son-in-law, Louis Riel, the Métis declared they would trade their furs wherever they pleased.

French-Canadian missionaries had come from Lower Canada to serve the Catholic Métis. In 1858 one of them, Bishop Alexandre Taché, invited Louis Riel's son, also called Louis, to travel back to Montreal. Young Louis was a bright lad, and the bishop thought that, with a proper education, he might make a good priest. So young Louis, Marie-Anne Lagimodière's grandson, went east to study.

No matter what boundary lines Britain and the United States had drawn on the map, the West belonged to the Métis, Blackfoot, Cree, and Assiniboine. For generations they had ridden the plains on horseback, fighting fast, violent battles and organizing exciting buffalo hunts. They were determined that no one would drive them from their territory. If Canada and its land-hungry settlers wanted the West, Canada would have to talk to the Métis and to the people of the buffalo.

But the buffalo were being hunted out of existence. The herds began to shrink in the 1860s. Soon the Plains Cree could find none of the animals in their hunting range. They grew angry at the Métis hunters and at intruders like the English lord who came to hunt buffalo simply for sport; one chief asked why he would come so far to kill the animals that sustained the Cree people. Soon the Cree had to ride farther west in search of buffalo herds. When they entered Blackfoot land, the long friendship of Cree and Blackfoot ended.

Maskepetoon of the Plains Cree believed that his people and the Blackfoot should not fight. He was a wise and much-travelled leader; he had met an American president in Washington, D.C., and had visited Vancouver Island, where he had ridden on the Hudson's Bay Company steamship *Beaver*. Now he tried to stop the war by the bravest deed a plains warrior could perform. In 1869 he rode unarmed into a Blackfoot camp to offer peace. The Blackfoot would either accept his offer – or kill him.

Some pictographs may be thousands of years old, while others come from more recent times. This one of a buffalo hunt on horseback was drawn in 1897.

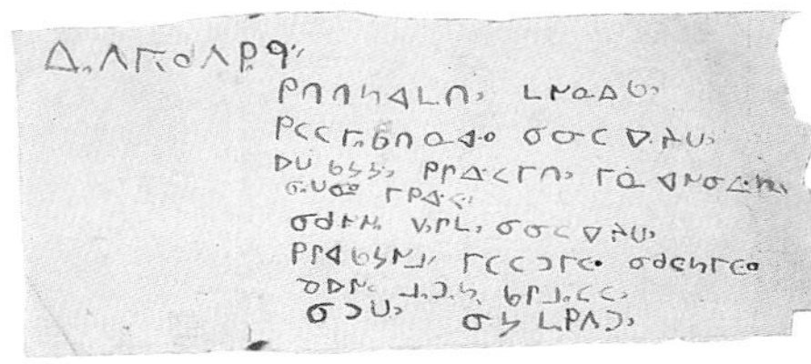

Cree traders and Protestant missionaries developed syllabics as a way to write the Cree language. This letter from Maskepetoon, the Cree grand chief, says: "He-who-speaks-from-above, I send you a letter. I shake hands with you. I want you to be here, to see you, I and the Assiniboines. There are twenty lodges. My son Benjamin, I want him to speak English. There are 164 buffalo. I tell you the news, my friend. I am Maskepetoon."

Trapped in the ice at Mercy Bay in the High Arctic while searching for Franklin, Captain Robert McClure abandoned HMS Investigator *in the winter of 1852.*

John Franklin's Tragic Quest

Was there really a Northwest Passage over the top of North America? By 1845, sailors and mapmakers knew that, if there was, it must be locked in ice most of the year, and thus quite useless to sailors. But no one actually knew what straits and passages might lie in Canada's frozen North. That year, Captain John Franklin set out to solve the last great mystery of northern exploration.

The British navy gave him 134 men and two ships, *Erebus* and *Terror*. They carried the best the navy could provide. There was steam heat and canned food (a new invention). The officers dined off fine china and drank from crystal goblets. They even had a grand piano. In July,

Maskepetoon knew that the Blackfoot and the Cree had been good friends. In past times, Cree warriors had helped the Blackfoot drive their enemies out of their hunting territories. But now both nations were desperate for buffalo. When Maskepetoon came in unarmed, the Blackfoot refused his offer of peace. One of their chiefs killed him, and the war went on.

The next year, 700 Cree warriors rode west to hunt buffalo on Blackfoot territory and to avenge their chief. By the Oldman River they met the Blackfoot. The Cree outnumbered the Blackfoot, and they spurred their horses forward to attack. The Blackfoot, however, had rifles, and they shot down the Cree horsemen. When the Cree fell back, the Blackfoot rushed across the river and surrounded them in a grove of trees. Hundreds of Cree died that day, and the Cree nation asked for peace.

The Battle of the Oldman was the last clash of the

Franklin and his men waved goodbye to whaling ships in Davis Strait. Then they sailed into the Northwest Passage – and never came out again.

It took years before the world learned Franklin's fate. As the British navy searched for him, it mapped most of the straits and islands of the Arctic Sea. There was indeed a passage between the islands, they learned – and Franklin had nearly found it when his ships had become trapped in the ice.

In 1854, Dr. John Rae, who travelled light and lived as the Inuit did, finally learned how and why Franklin's men had perished. Inuit hunters told him that Franklin's men had died, cold and starving, trying desperately to walk south to safety, until they had fallen in their tracks.

In Britain, Franklin and his men were mourned as tragic heroes of Arctic exploration. But John Rae realized that Franklin had tried to defeat the Arctic instead of living with it. To survive in the Arctic, explorers had to learn from the Inuit, who had been prospering there for a thousand years.

Young sailor John Torrington, just twenty, died on New Year's Day 1846, before the ill-fated Franklin expedition really got started. His shipmates buried him on Beechey Island. In 1984, 138 years later, scientists dug up his body, to see if lead poisoning from canned food had helped to doom the expedition. They found enough lead in Torrington to kill anyone.

plains warriors. The horseback nations had been weakened by epidemics, by the wars, and above all by the scarcity of the buffalo. Among the Blackfoot and the Cree, new leaders came forward to make peace. Crowfoot of the Blackfoot adopted Poundmaker of the Cree, and the two men urged the plains nations to stand together. They knew they must unite to face the power of the settlers who were moving into their land.

The Métis also suffered. The buffalo were disappearing, and at the same time English-speaking settlers were starting to arrive at Red River from the East. To face these challenges, the Métis needed strong leaders. The Métis council turned to young Louis Riel, Marie-Anne Lagimodière's grandson, who was just back from his schooldays in Montreal, and to master-hunter Gabriel Dumont. A new generation of leaders was stepping forth in the West.

Chapter 2

Mountains and Oceans

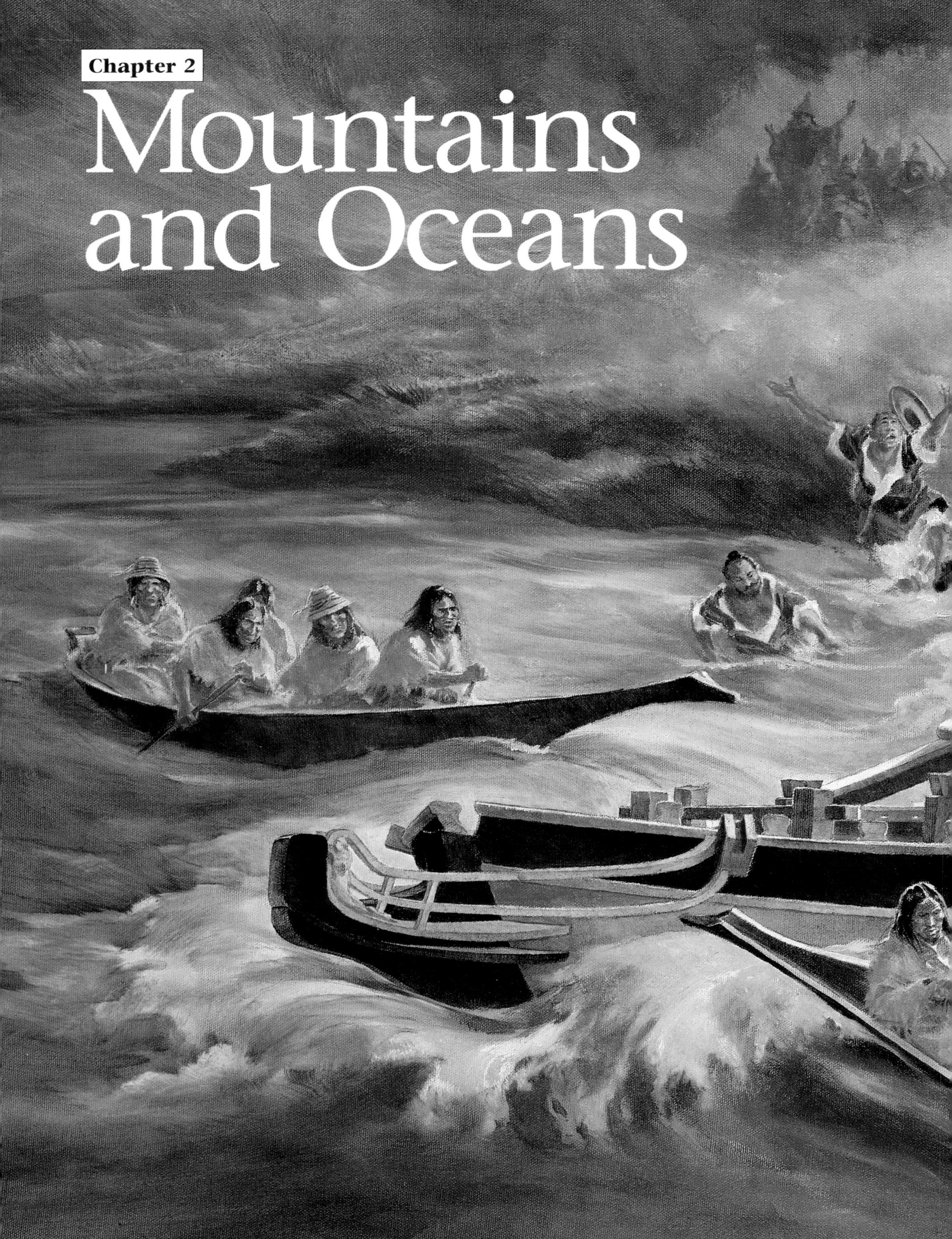

BETWEEN THE MOUNTAINS AND THE OCEAN, LONG GREEN STREAMERS of kelp floated in a cove called Yuquot, on the northwest coast of North America. Families of sea otters swam in the kelp. The sea otters were strong, lively swimmers, and the cold water never penetrated their thick, velvety-black fur. When the people of Yuquot needed winter cloaks, they hunted the sea otters. Their chief, Maquinna, wore handsome robes of sea-otter pelts.

In about 1740, Russian fur traders sailed across the narrow strait from Siberia to Alaska. Their leader, a Danish sailor named Vitus Bering, died miserably of scurvy on a bleak Alaskan island. The czars soon sent more expeditions across the strait, however, and the coast of Alaska became a Russian colony. From a forlorn outpost called New Archangel, Russian traders sent back sea-otter pelts gathered by the Aleut and Tlingit people. Rumours of these Russian traders reached the Spanish colony in Mexico, and in 1774 Juan Pérez Hernández sailed north to investigate. He landed and met the Native people of the northwest coast.

Four years later a British naval officer, Captain James Cook, came to the coast. In 1759, as an unknown young navigator, Cook had guided the British invasion fleet up the St. Lawrence to Quebec. Since then he had explored the world on sea voyages that had lasted years. Cook had already been to Australia, New Zealand, the islands of the Pacific, and the Antarctic seas. Now he was following the Russians and the Spanish to the northwest coast. He was chasing the old dream of a Northwest Passage, but looking for it from the opposite side. If a western entrance to such a passage lay on the misty northwest coast, Britain wanted to find it.

In the spring of 1778, James Cook stood on the quarterdeck as his ship, HMS *Resolution*, approached the coast near Yuquot Cove. The people who lived there sped out in their canoes to greet this strange, white-winged ship, and Cook spent a month at Yuquot. He gave Yuquot Cove the name Nootka, thinking that was what the local people called it. As his men repaired their ships, they talked and traded with the people. The Yuquot people admired the

Previous pages:
Enterprising seaman John Meares bought sea otter pelts in the Pacific Northwest and sold them in China. Sensing a good business, Meares brought back Chinese labourers, who built the ship North West America. *In the picture, Meares launches the ship at Nootka, on September 20, 1789, while Maquinna watches from the shore.*

Whalers return from the hunt.

iron tools the sailors carried, and in exchange for them they offered their gleaming sea-otter cloaks.

That summer Cook sailed north from Yuquot to Bering Strait, but he found no Northwest Passage. HMS *Resolution* sailed back to Hawaii for the winter months, and there Cook got into a fight with the local people and was killed. Cook's crew sailed on across the Pacific, and at Canton (now renamed Guangzhou), in China, they discovered that Chinese dignitaries would pay huge sums to have their robes trimmed with sea-otter fur. Sailors who had brought a few pelts along to use as blankets were suddenly rich.

The seashore at low tide was the food store of British Columbia's coastal nations. Along the shore at Nootka, a woman is gathering mussels; others fish or dig for clams. Details: *a rain hat woven from cedar bark, a halibut hook, and a soul-catcher – used to cure those plagued by evil spirits.*

The Nootka Traders

Nootka soon appeared on the maps of the world, as merchant ships from London, Boston, and Canton set course for the northwest coast. Among them was the *Imperial Eagle*, which carried a seventeen-year-old Englishwoman, Frances Barkley. She had just married the ship's captain, a globe-trotting merchant sailor named Charles William Barkley, and the seven-month voyage from Europe to Nootka was to be their honeymoon.

The Barkleys visited Nootka in 1787 and gave their names to nearby Barkley Sound and Frances Island. Frances loved the mild climate, and she admired the people there and the power and dignity of their chiefs. At Nootka the Barkleys met Maquinna, who received them wearing his magnificent cloak. Maquinna and his people were accustomed to trading ships by this time, and Captain Barkley was able to carry away a cargo of sea-otter pelts. The *Imperial Eagle* sailed to China and on around the world to Britain. The next time Captain Barkley sailed for Nootka, friends told Frances it was not proper for a wife and mother to go on sea voyages, but she refused to be left behind. She visited Nootka again in 1792, on her second trip around the world.

Many other European ships and sailors visited the northwest coast. In 1789, Captain John Meares brought thirty Chinese labourers who built a ship for him at Nootka – perhaps the first Chinese to visit North America since the time of Hwui Shin, who, some believe, came 1300 years before. Though men like Meares and Barkley came to trade, they did not always come peacefully. Sailors who distrusted the Native people attacked or abused them. Sometimes they turned their cannon on Native villages. The people of the coast struck back.

The Voyage to Fu Sang

Fu Sang was a land far from China. To go there meant a voyage of 20000 *li*, in the direction of the rising sun. Yet Hwui Shin set out to teach the people of Fu Sang about the Buddha.

In the year named Everlasting Origin – 499 by our calendar – Hwui Shin returned from Fu Sang and told amazing stories. The people of Fu Sang lived in houses made of planks, he said. They made their clothing from the bark of trees and were led by kings who ruled with great ceremony. Hwui Shin had travelled and preached among them before returning to China.

Perhaps Hwui Shin only sailed to Japan or to eastern Asia and found Fu Sang there. The story of Fu Sang may even have been a fable about the home from which the sun rose each morning. But Fu Sang may also have been the northwest coast of Canada. Chinese navigators may have crossed the Pacific Ocean fifteen centuries ago.

Age-old ties join the two continents of the North Pacific. In their seagoing canoes, the skilled sailors of British Columbia visited Alaska. Alaskan peoples, in turn, visited their neighbours in the Aleutian Islands, and the Aleutian people travelled across to Siberia. Everywhere they went, people traded goods and ideas and even styles of dress. The people of the northwest coast could have known about China even if Hwui Shin never reached them.

Still, it is exciting to imagine a Chinese junk with a crew of Buddhists threading its way through the misty islands and fiords and finding a welcome in the cedar villages.

Paul Kane is most famous for his paintings of buffalo hunters on the plains, but the wandering artist travelled on to the northwest coast, where he painted Clal-lum Women Weaving Blankets.

People of the Salmon

The people of the northwest coast were like no others in North America. They lived in a world of mountains, and rivers that cut deep channels through them – a world of islands and inlets and steep-sided fiords. Rainclouds rolled in from the Pacific Ocean to nurture a lush green rainforest. Colossal cedar and fir trees, a thousand years old, grew a hundred metres tall, towering over a thick undergrowth of ferns, salal, and broom.

The bays and rivers were rich with life. Halibut and whales, seals and otters swam in the sea, and each falling tide revealed shellfish on every rock and reef. Fat salmon swam up the rivers in summer. Returning from the ocean to spawn and die in the streams where they had been born, they came in such numbers that it seemed you could walk across the rivers on their backs.

The people of the coast lived on the wealth of the rainforest and the ocean. They felled the giant red cedars and split them into timbers and planks for their strong wooden houses. They carved totem poles over their doorways to honour the family's guardian spirits. Skilled carvers made many useful items – boxes and baskets and bowls and spoons – from cedar wood. Weavers and clothmakers made cedar branches into rope, and they pounded cedar bark into a kind of cloth. Hides and leather soon grew soft and rotted in the rainforest, but cedar-bark clothes and hats kept out the rain.

The west-coast people hollowed out cedar logs to make graceful canoes with high prows carved with intricate designs. In the biggest ones, which could carry fifty paddlers, they hunted whales in the open ocean. They also used the canoes to travel the twisting waterways from winter villages to summer fishing camps, and for trading and fishing.

Men went to war in these canoes, too. There were many nations living along the coast, speaking seventeen different languages, and wars among them were common. The Gitksan warrior Nekt lived in a hilltop fortress above the Skeena River. The Haida of the Queen Charlotte Islands went raiding far to the north and south, and distant people feared the sight of their long, sleek canoes.

The rainforest people lived from the salmon, as the plains people lived from the buffalo and the corngrowers from their fertile fields. Where the rivers roared through the steep mountain passes, they harpooned, netted, and

Terrible epidemics stalked the Haida people of the Queen Charlotte Islands in the 1860s. The few survivors had to abandon many of their ancient towns. Skidegate was one of only two towns that remained. Scientist George M. Dawson photographed it in 1878.

Ninstints

Out beyond the British Columbia coast lie the misty Queen Charlotte Islands. They are the homeland of the Haida nation, who call these islands Haida Gwaii.

The war canoes of the Haida once cut through the waters of the Pacific Northwest. The Haida villages were in protected coves close to fishing grounds and reefs rich with shellfish. At Kiusta, Skedans, Tanu, and the other villages, large houses built of cedar planks stood in a row facing the beach. Over the doorways or standing in front of the houses rose forests of totem poles.

One of the Haida's most important villages was Ninstints, on Anthony Island ("Skungwai" to the Haida), near the southern end of the Queen Charlottes. Ninstints was a busy place for thousands of years. But Ninstints, along with most of the Haida villages, was abandoned in the late 1800s.

Today Anthony Island is quiet, and only the totem poles remain. Ninstints has the finest array of totem poles still standing anywhere on the west coast. The United Nations has proclaimed Ninstints a World Heritage Site, one of the treasures of world civilization.

trapped enough salmon in a few frenzied weeks to feed themselves for a year. And because they were skilled at smoking salmon until it was hard and dry, their catch would keep all year round.

Salmon made the rainforest people wealthy. The wealthiest among them were the families of the chiefs, who commanded the best fishing spots. A chief had great power. He was richly dressed. He rode in a spectacular canoe, and he lived in a magnificent cedar house whose house poles boasted of great ancestors and guardian spirits. But chieftainship was a great burden. A chief had to guide his people, lead them in war, keep them well fed, and protect them from their enemies.

A chief proved his wealth and his generosity in a *potlatch*, a feast and ceremony where he gave gifts to all those who honoured and followed him, to prove his greatness. His family and all those close to him shared his honour and held high rank. The lowest-ranked people were merely slaves, for on this coast chiefs had slaves to serve them. The people of the woodlands and the plains owned little and believed all were equal, but the rainforest people owned much and knew just what rank they held in their society.

A chief like Maquinna would tolerate no insult to his people, or to himself. When visitors came to Yuquot in their big ships, he demanded respect. The arrogance of the traders often infuriated him. In 1803, after Captain Salter of the *Boston* insulted him, Maquinna seized the brig and chopped off the heads of the captain and his crew. He spared only John Jewitt, a young armourer on his first voyage, and an older man, John Thompson. He made them his slaves. Jewitt could repair tools and forge steel harpoons for Maquinna's whaling voyages. He became a valued member of the chief's household, and he saved Thompson's life by pretending that the old sailor was his father. The prisoners spent two years among the Yuquot people. By the time they were finally ransomed, Jewitt had learned to admire Maquinna, and he understood the chief's pride and anger. Still, he was glad to be going home!

This secret-society mask representing the sun was carved in the early 1900s by a Southern Kwakiutl artist. The tradition of carving these beautiful masks reaches back thousands of years and still continues. Today Native societies are recovering some of them from museums and collectors.

Despite the skirmishes and even the killings, sea captains and the coastal people continued to trade sea-otter pelts for copper and iron. Traders grew rich, Chinese mandarins luxuriated in furs, and rainforest villages acquired new tools. Only the sea otters lost out. In a few years they vanished from the coves and kelp beds of the northwest coast, driven almost to extinction by the trade in their pelts.

Not all the quarrels on the coast were between traders and Native chiefs. The Spanish and English empires clashed there. For centuries Spain, which had colonies from Chile and Mexico to the Philippines, had considered the Pacific Ocean its private ocean. After Captain Cook sailed to

Nootka, the Spanish governor in Mexico sent many expeditions to lay claim to the northwest coast. Estevan, Alberni, Galiano, Langara, and many other Spanish captains left their names scattered over the maps of the coasts they explored. But when they built a fort at Nootka in 1789 and began seizing British ships, the British talked of war.

In the end, Spain and Britain agreed not to fight over Nootka, and the British sent Captain George Vancouver to Nootka in HMS *Discovery*. In 1792, Vancouver met Spain's Captain Quadra there, and they settled the Nootka dispute. Then Vancouver – who had been part of Cook's crew in 1778 – set out to complete Cook's explorations of the northwest coast.

In 1789, Britain's Royal Navy chose an officer named Roberts to lead its expedition to the Pacific Northwest. At the last moment he could not go, and Captain George Vancouver was sent instead. Nearly a century later, William Van Horne of the CPR named the railway's western terminus after Vancouver. Might the city have been called Roberts or Robertsville?

Vancouver wanted to settle whether the Northwest Passage really existed. For three summers his ships and boats crawled in and out of the passages and inlets of the coast, charting and mapping, but found no channel that opened up to lead them through the continent. The notion of a Northwest Passage had tantalized navigators for nearly three hundred years, but Vancouver proved that, if any sea route around North America existed, it surely lay in the far and frozen North.

From Canada, by Land

In June 1793, Captain Vancouver's boat crews explored an inlet they named Dean Channel, near Bella Coola. If they had lingered just six weeks longer, they might have made a spectacular rendezvous. For another explorer visited Bella Coola and the Dean Channel in July. Alexander Mackenzie reached there by canoe and on foot, from far-distant Montreal.

Mackenzie was one of the North West Company trailblazers who had peppered the woodlands with trading forts all the way to the Rocky Mountains, until the western ocean seemed within reach. Alexander Mackenzie decided to strike for the Pacific.

A single canoe carried Alexander Mackenzie and nine men all the way to British Columbia. To reach the Pacific, however, they had to leave the canoe and walk through the mountains to the sea.

His first venture mistakenly led him north to the Arctic Ocean, not west to the Pacific. The river he discovered was later named for him, but Mackenzie was disappointed. He went to Britain to learn more about surveying and mapmaking, and in 1793 he was ready to start again. He crammed ten men with all their gear and weapons into a single trading canoe and headed for the mountains.

Mackenzie and his voyageurs fought their way up and down wild rivers and through canyons, and hauled their boat and all their supplies across portages. Mackenzie wanted to stay on the rivers, but the Carrier people he met persuaded him to change his plans. They warned him that the rivers were murderous, and told him they had a good overland trail they used to bring fish oil up from the coast. Mackenzie and his men left their canoe behind and set off to walk this "Grease Trail" down to the ocean. On July 22, 1793, on a flat rock on the edge of Dean Channel, he wrote a message in red dye mixed with grease: "Alexander Mackenzie, from Canada, by land." With the ghosts of Champlain, La Salle, and La Vérendrye looking over his shoulders, he had reached the western ocean.

Alexander Mackenzie used fish grease and red dye to leave this message on the rocks at Bella Coola in 1793. Today, the words are carved and painted, a permanent monument to his journey.

David Thompson: Mapmaker of the West

Because British Columbia's rugged mountains block the horizon, David Thompson sights his sextant on an "artificial horizon" to measure his position. Pouring liquid mercury from an iron bottle into a flat tray, he produces an absolutely level surface, and sights on it.

"I have fully completed the survey of this part of North America from sea to sea," he wrote later, "and by almost innumerable astronomical observations have determined the positions of the mountains, lakes and rivers, and other remarkable places on the northern part of this continent."

Thompson never performed one single great feat of exploration like those of Alexander Mackenzie or Simon Fraser. Instead, he explored the mountain labyrinths of British Columbia for years, and while others simply travelled through the mountain passes, Thompson made sense of them.

Thompson began as a poor boy from England, apprenticed to the Hudson's Bay Company at the age of fourteen. He roamed the Prairies and learned Cree and Peigan. He admired the Native people, and he lived happily with his Métis wife, Charlotte, for sixty years. But he was an unusual fur trader, because he was devoutly religious and he wouldn't drink alcohol.

In 1790, laid up at the Hudson's Bay post of Cumberland House with a broken leg (and going blind in one eye), the twenty-year-old Thompson learned both mapmaking and geographical surveying. After doing surveys for the Hudson's Bay Company, he joined the Nor'Westers, who set him to exploring

and mapping the vast territory from Lake Superior to the Pacific. He would be a mapmaker for the rest of his working life.

Thompson died in 1857, old, blind, and forgotten. In his later years he had laboured over a narrative of his western journeys, based on the careful journals he had kept wherever he travelled. This is his description of how his expedition got caught in a blizzard in what is now southwestern Manitoba, in December 1797.

At 7½ AM our bit of a caravan set off; as the Dogs were fresh, we walked at a good pace for some time; a gentle south wind arose; and kept increasing; by 10 AM it was a heavy Gale, with high drift and dark weather, so much so that I had to keep the Compass in my hand, for I could not trust to the Wind. By Noon, it was a perfect Storm, we had no alternative but to proceed, which we did slowly and with great labour, for the Storm was ahead, and the snow drift in our faces. Night came on, I could no longer see the Compass, and had to trust to the Wind; the weather became mild with small rain, but the Storm continued with darkness; some of the foremost called to lie down where we were, but as it was evident we were ascending a gentle rising ground, we continued and soon, thank good Providence, my face struck against some Oak saplings, and I passed the word that we were in the Woods, a fire was quickly made, and as it was on an elevated place it was seen afar off. As yet the only one with me, was my servant who led the Horse and we anxiously awaited the others; they came hardly able to move, one, and then another, and in something more than half an hour, nine had arrived; each with Dogs, and Sleds, but one Man, and a Sled with the Dogs were missing; to search for the latter was useless; but how to find the former, we were at a loss: and remained so for another half an hour, when we thought we heard his voice, the Storm was still rageing, we extended ourselves within call of each other, the most distant man heard him plainly, went to him, raised him up, and with assistance brought him to the fire, and we all thanked the Almighty for our preservation. He told us he became weak, fell several times, and at length he could not get up, and resigned himself to perish in the storm, when by chance lifting up his head he saw the fire, this gave him courage; stand he could not but [he] shuffled away on hands and knees through the snow, bawling with all his might until we fortunately heard him. We threw the Tent over some Oak sapplings and got under shelter from showers of rain, hail and sleet: at 7½ PM Ther 36 being four degrees above the freezing point; by a south wind making in little more than twelve hours a difference of temperature of fifty six degrees. I had weathered many a hard gale, but this was the most distressing day I had ever seen.

The people by the ocean told Mackenzie they had recently been visited by a sailor they called Macubah – George Vancouver. But Mackenzie went home discouraged, even though he wrote a wonderful book about his travels and was knighted by the British king. Furs were Mackenzie's business, and the North West Company was not interested in the western ocean unless their voyageurs and canoes could follow a river to it.

The Nor'Westers returned to the western mountains in 1805. Simon Fraser was a tough young explorer whose Loyalist father had died in a rebel prison during the American Revolution. Deep in the mountain country west of the Rockies, which he named New Caledonia (from an old Latin name for Scotland), he built Fort George. Soon he began sending canoes laden with furs on the long haul back to Montreal. Like Mackenzie before him, Fraser hungered for the glory of finding a river route to the Pacific. Already sailors on the northwest coast had visited the mouth of a river they called the Columbia. Fraser hoped his Fort George stood on the banks of the same river. In May 1808, he launched his canoes to find out.

Soon Fraser and his men were plunged into terrifying rapids. The Native people of the valley urged him to take the footpath across the heights instead. But Fraser stayed on his river, even though the voyage became a nightmare. "I have been for a long time among the Rocky Mountains," he wrote in his diary, "but have never seen anything equal to this country. We had to pass where no human being should venture."

The men finally cached their canoes in a safe place and followed the river on "a kind of beaten path used by the natives, and made passable by means of scaffolds, bridges, and ladders." Fraser's Native guides climbed nimbly along swaying ladders, like sailors in the rigging of a tall ship. The explorers had no choice but to follow, and after a hundred close calls they got through the canyon. On July 2, 1808, Fraser reached the Pacific Ocean.

Like Mackenzie, Simon Fraser went home disappointed. His river – it was named for him later – was too

"We had to pass where no human being should venture," noted Simon Fraser about his struggle through the Fraser canyon. "We would never have got through if the Natives had not aided us," declared Jules Quesnel, who went with him.

wild and treacherous for fur traders, and it reached the ocean too far north to be the Columbia. Fraser said he would never have made the voyage if he had known how it would turn out. For another fifty years, the northwest coast turned its face only to the sea.

The Father of British Columbia

After Mackenzie and Fraser, few voyageurs made the long canoe trip from Montreal to New Caledonia. Although there were furs to be had there, it was easier to send them out by sea. Both Nor'Westers and Baymen began building trading posts along the coast. The Hudson's Bay Company put a fort near the mouth of the Columbia River and sent sailing ships up and down the coast. From the Columbia, the ships sailed across the oceans to Canton or London.

Spain no longer challenged British trade on the northwest coast, but the United States did. American settlers began moving into the Oregon country nearby. They were eager to drive the Hudson's Bay Company forts from the Columbia River, and they looked north, all the way to the Russian traders in Alaska. Perhaps the United States and the Russians would meet at latitude 54°40'N, squeezing out the Hudson's Bay Company and its British colony.

In 1843, James Douglas rode the Hudson's Bay

Opposite:
At Fort Victoria in 1843, James Douglas supervises as the Hudson's Bay Company steamship Beaver *unloads a horse along with other supplies.*

Company steamship *Beaver* into a sheltered harbour on the southern tip of Vancouver Island. It seemed to him "a perfect Eden," and he set about building a trading post there. He named it Victoria in honour of the young queen. A few years later, Britain yielded the Oregon country to the United States, but the coast from the forty-ninth parallel north to Russian Alaska remained British. Fort Victoria, which replaced the Columbia River trading posts, became the capital of the little colony called Vancouver Island. By 1851, James Douglas, chief factor of the Hudson's Bay Company on Vancouver Island, was also the queen's royal governor there.

"Old Squaretoes" was cold, formal, and aloof, and he made few friends. But everyone respected him. He had been a fur trader since his teens. Now he was almost fifty, a tall, powerful man with a grim stare. Like most of the settlers of his new colony, he came from far away. He had been born in the West Indies. His Scots father was a plantation owner; his mother's African ancestors had been slaves. After joining the Hudson's Bay Company, Douglas had married a half-Native woman, Amelia Connolly. Unlike

Steaming Up the Silent Fiords

In July 1836, the steamship *Beaver* came churning and rattling through the steep-sided channels of the northwest coast. Its paddle wheels streamed a broad wake behind the ship, and its smokestack billowed a tall white plume overhead. A team of axemen needed two days to cut enough wood to fuel the *Beaver*'s boilers for a day, but, for the first time, the beat of an engine echoed along the coast.

Unlike the sailing ships that had come before, the *Beaver* could slip in and out of every narrow creek and sheltered cove, in contrary winds or no winds at all. It made the northwest coast a little outpost of the Hudson's Bay Company and the British empire. The Baymen drove all competition from the coast, and the *Beaver* helped them do it.

Barely fifty years before the *Beaver*, the first sailing ships had appeared on the coast. By the time the steamship was wrecked at the entrance to Vancouver's harbour in 1888, the Hudson's Bay Company's Pacific outpost had grown into a proud province of Canada.

Lady Amelia and Sir James Douglas.

many fur traders, he did not disown her when he became wealthy and important. Douglas dared any British-born people to insult his origins or his wife's.

Douglas intended to see a colony grow around the little outpost at Victoria. He encouraged sawmilling, salmon fishing, and mining, and tried to attract farmers. People came from all directions. Some came from England and sailed round South America's Cape Horn, and others came up the coast from California. Chinese labourers and Hawaiian Islanders came across the Pacific. There were even a few settlers from distant Canada.

The Native people of the rainforest were still powerful and independent, and their fleets of war canoes still sailed the coastal waters. They far outnumbered the handful of settlers on Vancouver Island. When a settler at Barkley Sound told the Nootka chiefs that "King George's men" – as the British were still called, even after Victoria became queen – would pay the Native people for their land and take care of them, the chiefs replied, "We do not wish to sell our land nor our water. Let your friends stay in their own country."

But British settlers continued to arrive. Once more, disease travelled with the newcomers, and dreadful epidemics swept along the coast, killing thousands of Native people. Villages that had been bustling communities for centuries suddenly stood empty, and the forest crept over them. The power that chiefs like Maquinna had wielded so proudly began to shift to the newcomers. Governor Douglas demanded that the Native nations accept British law. Once, armed with only a cutlass, he sat all day facing 200 angry Cowichans, until they surrendered a man who had killed a settler.

All the same, Douglas's colony was still a very small place on the edge of the world. Victoria had only 700 people in 1858. Then something changed the northwest coast for ever. It was gold.

The Gold Fields

In the 1850s, gold fever was making the world seem a smaller place. Gold seekers had rushed to California in 1849 and to Australia in 1851. A few who were early or lucky got rich fast. The rest never found enough gold to pay for their shovels and pans, and they moved on, looking for a new strike. In 1849 the "Forty-Niners" had transformed California from a faraway outpost of Spain into a state of the United States. Within a few years, many of them were broke and looking for new goldfields.

Then bright flakes of gold turned up in sluices and pans along the sandbars where the Thompson River runs into the Fraser. In April 1858, the paddle-wheel steamship *Commodore* arrived in Victoria from California, its decks crowded with excited men wearing the trademark red flannel shirts of gold-rush miners. By the end of the year, some 20000 miners had passed through Victoria to seek their fortune on the Fraser. Soon prospectors had staked every sandbar on the Fraser.

The gold rush gave James Douglas a new challenge, and he acted swiftly. Though he was governor of only Vancouver Island, he took charge of the mainland too, imposing British rule and British law. When the distant government in London heard of his action, they approved. The mainland became the colony of British Columbia,

The Hudson's Bay trading post at Nanaimo on Vancouver Island became a busy place after coal was discovered there in 1852. The coal miners' labour made a fortune for mine-owner Robert Dunsmuir, who moved to Victoria and built a castle for his family.

named by Queen Victoria herself, and James Douglas became governor of British Columbia as well.

Douglas imposed order on the goldfields and the miners, and soon even bewildered Californians were giving three cheers for Queen Victoria by the banks of the Fraser. Judge Matthew Begbie arrived from England to administer stern British justice in the wild gold-rush shantytowns. Once, when a jury acquitted a man accused of murder, Judge Begbie called the jurymen a pack of horse thieves and said he wished he could hang *them*. When a tough miner named Ned McGowan declared that he was the king of Hills' Bar and told Governor Douglas to leave him alone, Colonel Richard Moody's Royal Engineers marched in and persuaded him to salute the Union Jack.

In 1859, Colonel Moody began clearing the forest for a town called New Westminster, to be the capital of the mainland colony. The Royal Engineers also built roads and trails along the rivers and through the mountain passes. Their greatest project was the Great North Road to the Cariboo country. The miners knew that the Fraser River gold had washed down from somewhere else, and they kept pushing north in search of the mother lode. In 1861 a Cornish sailor named Billy Barker struck gold in the Cariboo country, and the fading excitement of the Fraser River rush revived. Douglas sent the Royal Engineers scrambling through the mountain passes to build a road 650 kilometres long, much of it blasted out of solid rock, from Yale on the Fraser River to the heart of the Cariboo.

Someone had the bright idea that camels would be the perfect pack animals in the dry Cariboo country. Some of the camels escaped and went wild, but they could not survive the winters.

In Montreal, Toronto, and a hundred other eastern towns, news of the Fraser River gold strikes reminded people of Simon Fraser and his epic voyage. Now that Canada was looking west again, the old fur trader, who was living quietly near Cornwall in Canada West, became famous again as "the first discoverer of that golden stream." Young men from eastern farms and towns, including Fraser's own son, headed for the B.C. goldfields by land or sea.

The Overlanders, a group of men and one woman, Catherine Schubert (who joined the group with her husband and children), set out to cross the continent to the Cariboo. They chose Thomas McMicking, a young shopkeeper from Niagara, as their leader. The Overlanders faced a thousand perils and hardships as they crossed the Prairies in carts, but McMicking got the whole party to British Columbia. The day after they reached Kamloops, Catherine Schubert gave birth to a baby girl, Rose.

One man who earned a nickname and became a legend in the Cariboo was John Cameron, from Glengarry, Canada West. In 1861, when news of the Cariboo gold strike reached Glengarry, Cameron and his wife, Margaret, set off by sea to Victoria, then hiked up the Cariboo road to Barkerville. Cameron staked a claim on Williams Creek and kept a crew digging all summer and fall. In December came the bonanza: gold, in fabulous amounts! A town called Camerontown sprang up overnight. Cariboo Cameron found himself rich.

Rich but broken-hearted, because Margaret Cameron had died of typhoid fever in October. Cariboo had sworn then that he would take her back to Glengarry. A month after the big strike, he carried her sealed coffin to Victoria. Before the year was out, he had taken her home and buried her in the family plot.

Cameron settled in Glengarry with his money and married again, but jealous neighbours claimed he had brought home a coffin filled with gold, not his wife's body. To stop the rumours, Cariboo Cameron had to dig up Margaret and open her coffin. Then, disgusted with his neighbours, he moved back to British Columbia. By the time he died in Barkerville, his fortune was gone, and no one sent *his* body back home.

The gold miners had expanded the territory of British Columbia inland from the edge of the ocean. Already railways were spreading across the eastern half of the continent. Indeed, when John Palliser's exploring party had made its way into the Rocky Mountains in 1857, one of Palliser's scientists had actually spent some time calculating how a railway might run through the passes. One day it might be possible to cross the continent without the hardships of the voyageurs or the Overlanders.

Catherine Schubert, the only woman to travel overland across western Canada to the British Columbia goldfields, gave birth to a baby the day after she arrived at Kamloops, B.C.

Mister Deas Cans Fish

John Sullivan Deas's parents had been slaves in South Carolina. Young John learned the tinsmithing trade and went to the California gold rush of 1849, but then drifted north with other Black adventurers and began tinsmithing in Victoria in about 1861.

Captain Edward Stamp had started a salmon cannery on the Fraser River not far from New Westminster. The river ran thick with salmon every summer, and Stamp knew that, if he canned them, he could sell salmon all over the world. He hired John Deas to make tin cans. When Stamp suddenly died, Deas took over the cannery. Soon he was running the largest salmon canning business in the colony. Thousands of cases of John Deas's Fraser River salmon went off to Britain every year.

With a Black owner, Native fishermen supplying the salmon, and Chinese immigrants doing most of the labour, it was a remarkable multicultural business. But Deas was mocked and abused for the colour of his skin. The Natives were soon driven out of the fishing business, and the Chinese labourers suffered cruel discrimination. John Deas moved back to the United States and died young, probably poisoned by the mercury that tinsmiths used. Newer, bigger canneries replaced his, but his name lives on in Deas Island, at the mouth of the Fraser River.

Mountains and Oceans

Gold fever drew tens of thousands of people to British Columbia in the late 1850s and early 1860s. Within a few years the gold rush was over, but the colony continued to grow. In less than a lifetime, the rush of settlers and the cruel scourge of epidemics left the Native nations a dispossessed minority in their own land. In 1866, British Columbia and Vancouver Island united to form one colony. To the disgust of the mainlanders, Victoria became the capital, but the united colony took the name British Columbia.

The "father" of the colony, James Douglas, had retired,

honoured by Queen Victoria with a knighthood, in 1864. By the time he died in Victoria in 1877, the threat from the Americans seemed almost as faint as that from the Russians or the Spanish. The governor and his colonists had turned a land once known only to the Native nations and a few lonely traders into a thriving British colony.

Victoria had 6000 people and Barkerville nearly as many. There were newspapers in the towns, and a legislature full of squabbling politicians at Victoria. (The most colourful of the politicians was William Smith, who had come from Nova Scotia by way of California, and changed his name to Amor De Cosmos, "lover of the universe.") British naval vessels cruised the British Columbia waters, and merchant vessels from all over the world came and went. A tough Scots coal miner named Robert Dunsmuir was amassing a fortune from the coal mines of Nanaimo, while the miners, who risked life and limb for a meagre wage, cursed his name and went on strike whenever they could, for more money and more safety.

On Burrard Inlet, near New Westminster, Sewell Moody's sawmills cut lumber for California, Chile, and Australia, and a little community called Gastown sprouted around talkative "Gassy" Jack Deighton's hotel. On the Fraser River, John Deas's cannery was packing salmon for sale in England. Steamships churned up the Fraser to Yale, and stagecoaches and wagons rumbled along the road to Barkerville – where, in 1867, the Canadians cheered for Dominion Day on July first and the Americans celebrated Independence Day on July fourth. British Columbia was part of neither country; it was still a British colony.

"Who can see what the next ten years may bring forth?" wrote James Douglas in 1863. "A railroad on British territory, probably, from the Gulf of Georgia to the Atlantic." British Columbia had rooted itself on the shores of the ocean, and it still looked out to the sea. But it had pushed into inland valleys and was beginning to look eastward over the Rockies. From the other side of the mountains, Canada was looking west with new interest.

Susan Allison

Susan Moir was born in Ceylon and arrived in British Columbia with her family in 1860, when she was fifteen. In 1868 she married John Allison, a gold-rush miner who had turned to ranching. Long before other settlers moved inland, Susan went with him over the Allison Pass to the lovely Similkameen valley. She lived there for thirty years, confronting fires, rattlesnakes, outlaws, and wolves, and she raised fourteen children.

Later, in Vancouver, she wrote about that "wild, free life" and the Native people's stories of mysterious Bigmen in the mountains and the dangerous monster that swam in Lake Okanagan.

Chapter 3

Confederation Days

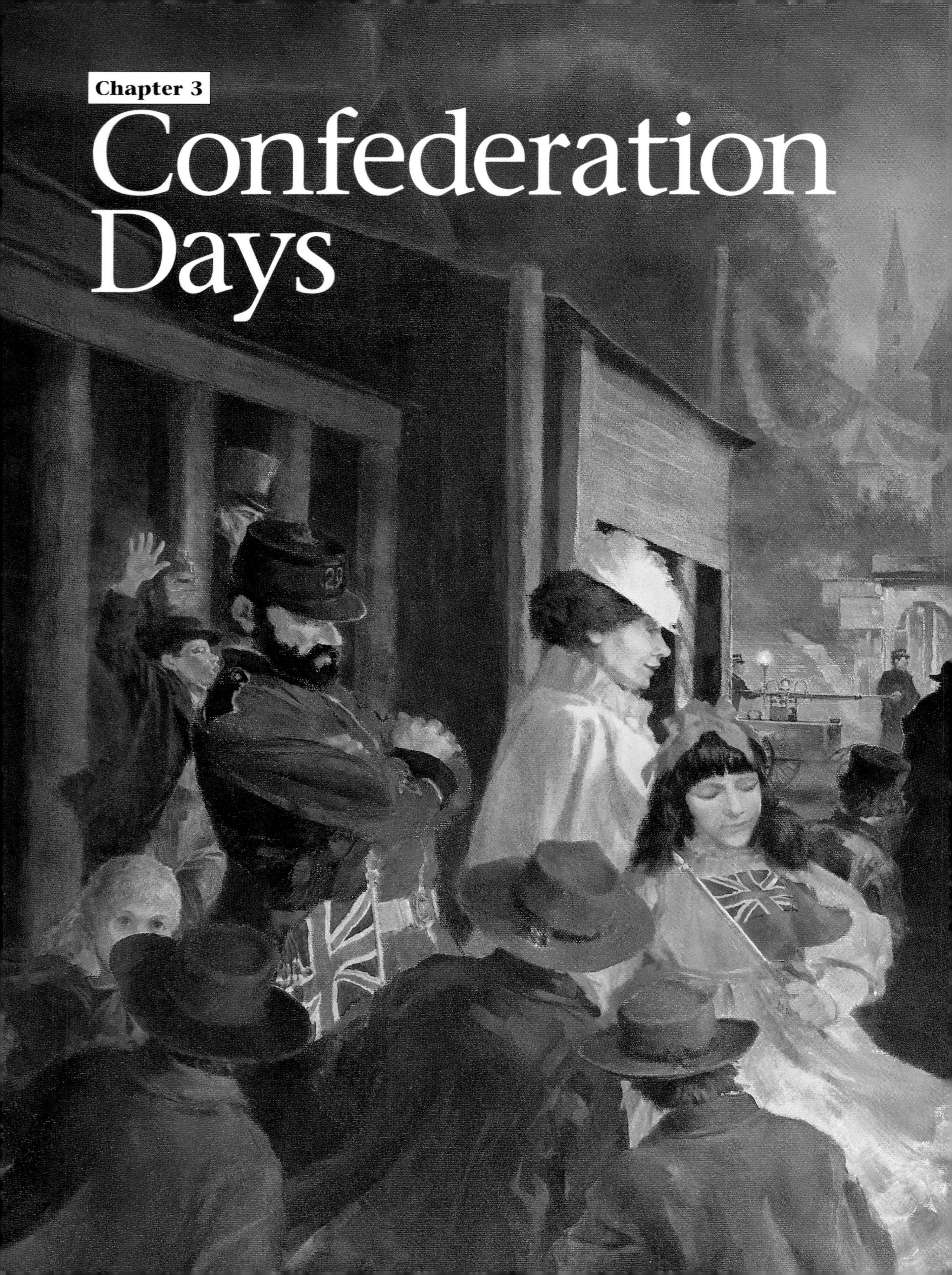

A.TYSON'S GROC
NOVA SCOTIA
CANADA WEST
CANADA EAST

THE 1860S WERE BUSY, EXCITING YEARS IN BRITISH NORTH AMERICA. Queen Victoria, who ruled Britain and its colonies, had been just eighteen when she had ascended the throne in 1837, but by the 1860s she seemed as permanent as the empire itself. After her beloved husband, Prince Albert, died in 1861, she always wore black, and she insisted that her courtiers at Windsor Castle wear black armbands. But the empire of "the widow of Windsor" was bigger and richer than ever, and British North America was proud to be part of it.

You could feel the excitement in the daily newspapers. There were 300 newspapers in British North America, and most towns had several. Halifax had nearly a dozen. For a penny or two a day, men and women could sit down in their comfortable parlours and keep up with the news. The news probably included some horrible crime or maybe a hanging, for newspaper writers, like some of their readers, could be bloodthirsty.

There was sure to be something about railways in the newspaper. Railway mania had possessed British North America ever since Canada's first train began running on flimsy wooden tracks laid near Montreal in 1836. By the 1860s, iron tracks crisscrossed the colonies. Belching smoke and showering sparks, steam locomotives roared through the night, drawing towns and colonies closer together. Newspapers were full of stories about new railway lines, new iron bridges, and new telegraph lines humming with news.

In the 1860s, many people still farmed. Others worked at dangerous jobs such as mining and earned barely enough to live. Even scrawny, underfed children worked twelve hours a day, with no laws to protect them. When the work was done, men and women – and sometimes children, too – drank raw whisky and played rowdy games to forget their troubles.

But other people in British North America had a different, more enjoyable life. They lived in comfortable houses, worshipped in handsome stone churches with soaring spires, and attended concert halls to hear a reading

Previous pages:
On July 1, 1867, the great Dominion Day torchlight parade marches past the intersections of King and Queen in Berlin (now Kitchener), Ontario. The New Hamburg militia lieutenant (left) *who is watching the volunteer firemen roll their new pumper has already marched in the military parade, held earlier in the day.*

When the Prince of Wales visited Ottawa in 1860, one of the amusements that was arranged for him was a ride down a timber slide.

by Charles Dickens, the English novelist, or a concert by Jenny Lind, "the Swedish nightingale." For them, British North America was a place of religion, proper manners, and temperance.

There was always news of politics in the papers. Britain still ruled its colonies, but on local matters the elected governments ran the affairs of each colony. In each one, the leader of the party with the most support in the elected Assembly became premier, and so the parties battled furiously for votes. In most of the colonies, voters had to stand up in public and declare which candidate they wanted. Supporters of other candidates shouted, threatened, and often stopped rivals from voting. Only men could vote, and most of them declared that women were represented by their fathers or husbands and had no need of their own votes. In fact, many men did not have a vote either; only those who owned enough property could qualify.

Many newspaper editors were also politicians – and an editor who wasn't in politics himself probably worked for an owner who was. George Brown, a tall, loud, redheaded

Follow the Drinking Gourd

Josiah and Charlotte Henson were slaves who laboured on the cotton plantations of Kentucky. One dark night in 1830, they gathered a small parcel of food and twenty-five cents (all the money they had), and fled north with their children. Josiah Henson carried his youngest children in a sack on his back.

The Henson family hid from slave-catchers by day and walked through woods and swamps at night. They were following the "drinking gourd," the Big Dipper. It pointed the way north to Canada, which had abolished slavery. The Hensons sang:

So long, old master,
Don't come after me,
I'm heading north to Canada
Where everyone is free.

Soon the Hensons got aboard the underground railroad. This wasn't really a railroad, just a network of people who hated slavery so much that they sheltered escaped slaves and helped them to reach Canada – often at great risk to themselves. When he crossed the Niagara River, Josiah Henson fell on his knees and kissed the earth.

The drinking gourd and the underground railroad led thousands of escaped slaves to Canada. Near Dresden, Upper Canada, Josiah and Charlotte Henson founded a Black community named Dawn. Mary Ann Shadd ran a newspaper and fought against the discrimination that Blacks suffered. Jack Little and his wife went into the woods "where any people might go, coloured or poor, and have a chance to settle the land." After fifteen years, the Littles were the proud owners of a thriving hundred-acre (forty-hectare) farm.

In 1861 a civil war broke out in the United States, between the northerners, who had now abolished slavery, and the southerners, who still depended on slaves. Many Blacks went back to fight on the northern side. When the North won the war, slavery was abolished throughout the United States.

Scotsman from Toronto, was one of those newspapermen-politicians. He was the publisher of *The Globe*, the most widely read paper in British North America, and he was also the leader of the Reformers of Canada West. He was a passionate, outspoken man, and his loves and hates helped bring a group of Canadian politicians to Charlottetown on a sunny day in 1864.

Breaking the Deadlock

George Brown loved his newspaper, his new wife, Anne, and their baby daughter, his Presbyterian church, and his political party, the reforming "Grits" of Canada West. He did not like Catholics or anything that struck him as anti-British, and he hated the way the people of Canada West were bound in union with the French Catholics of Canada East. In the Parliament of the United Canadas, the two halves of Canada had vetoed each other's plans and blocked each other's ambitions for years. This squabbling made Brown so angry that he talked of quitting politics.

Most of all, George Brown hated John A. Macdonald of the "Tories." Their two political parties had been rivals for years, but this was a personal battle too. They flung insults at each other in the Assembly of the United Canadas in Quebec City, and they opposed each other at every step. Brown could hardly stand to be in the same room as the slim, jaunty man everyone called "John A." To Brown's fury, John A. usually won their battles. With his ally George-Etienne Cartier, the leader of the "Bleu" party of Canada East, Macdonald kept George Brown out of power for years.

One steaming, humid day in June 1864, George Brown stood up in the Assembly of the United Canadas to make a startling offer. His Grits would join Macdonald's Tories and Cartier's Bleus, he announced. His Protestant followers from Canada West would work alongside the Catholic French of Canada East. He would even work with John A. Macdonald. There was one condition. No more petty politics! No more squabbling over Canada East and

In the 1860s, being photographed meant you had to sit absolutely still for several minutes, often with a brace holding your head steady. Perhaps that is why George Brown always looks long-faced and solemn in his photographs. In real life he was full of energy, brimming with enthusiasm one moment, fury the next.

Sir John A. Macdonald.

Canada West! They must work for a common cause, said Brown – the transformation of all of British North America into one nation.

Macdonald and Cartier agreed to work with Brown. But to achieve anything, the Canadians had to talk to the Maritimers as well. Barely two months after Brown's offer, the Canadian leaders set sail for Charlottetown, Prince Edward Island, where the Maritime politicians were meeting. So few of the Canadians had ever been to the Maritimes that one of them asked, "What kind of people are they?"

The Idea of Confederation

September 1, 1864, was a warm, sunny Thursday in Prince Edward Island. In those days Charlottetown was a pretty little town of barely 7000 people, but it was no sleepy backwater. It and all the other seaports of Atlantic Canada were busy places. Maritimers built and sailed a fleet of beautiful ships and schooners that hauled freight around the globe. In summer, Charlottetown harbour was a forest of masts, where trim sailing vessels loaded and unloaded and sailors caroused on shore.

This week, every hotel and boarding-house was crammed. The Olympic Circus was in town for a four-day

A four-horse team pulls a load of logs out of the woods. All through the nineteenth century, lumbering was the greatest industry in many parts of eastern Canada. Logs were dragged to the rivers in winter, and floated down to sawmills or seaports in the spring.

A man rakes oysters through the ice at Shediac, New Brunswick, in this painting by William Hind. Atlantic Canada's shellfish, today a gourmet specialty, were once harvested mostly as poor people's food.

run, and at the same time the leaders of the three Maritime colonies were holding a conference. Down on the dock, William Henry Pope was rushing about, trying to find a boat. Pope was a Cabinet minister in the government of Prince Edward Island, and he had distinguished guests to greet. Out in the bay, the steamship *Queen Victoria* had just anchored. The leading politicians from Canada were aboard – among them John A. Macdonald, George-Etienne Cartier, D'Arcy McGee, and George Brown. Finally, in desperation, Pope seized a filthy flat-bottomed scow, and an old fisherman rowed him out to meet his visitors.

The Canadians had not originally been expected at the Charlottetown Conference, which was supposed to discuss Maritime union – the joining of Prince Edward Island, Nova Scotia, and New Brunswick into a single colony. But that idea was going nowhere. The island's

premier, John Hamilton Gray, had said he did not mind adding New Brunswick and Nova Scotia to Prince Edward Island, but he certainly did not want Prince Edward Island added to the mainland!

Just when the chance for Maritime union seemed about to die, the Canadians arrived with a different suggestion: Why not unite *all* of British North America? It was a big, bold idea, and the Maritimers liked it. They put aside the plan of Maritime union and began to discuss the Canadian proposal. As the two groups worked together and got to know each other, the idea of Confederation seized them all.

Let us found a nation on the northern half of this continent, the men at Charlottetown said eagerly. From the Great Lakes to Newfoundland, Britain's North American

colonies were thriving and prosperous communities. Now the time seemed right for these colonies, each with its own traditions and dreams, to become provinces of a new nation. Because they would form a federal union, each province would run its own affairs – but there were many great things they could do together. There were railways to build, trade links to expand, bonds to forge against the American hunger to expand northward. The colonists felt ready to build a country.

The seed of Confederation was sown in those sunny September days at Charlottetown. But there were still a thousand details of this new nation to thrash out. The Charlottetown delegates agreed to meet again a month later, at Quebec.

Many of the Fathers of Confederation can be seen in this painting of a ball at Province House in Charlottetown. Making Confederation was not all meetings and work. At Charlottetown and Quebec, the politicians and their families and guests dined and danced whenever they could.

From Charlottetown to Quebec

Poor Mercy Ann Coles! All the way by ship and train from Charlottetown, she had been looking forward to the excitement of Quebec City. Her father, George Coles, was one of Prince Edward Island's delegates to the great Confederation conference, and dinners, dances, and sight-seeing tours were planned for the delegates and their families. Mercy Ann, who was seventeen, had brought her beautiful blue silk ballgown with her. But no sooner had they all arrived and the dances begun than Mercy Ann caught a fever.

For ten days she lay miserably in her bed, gazing out at the October rain. "I am sure I shall know the shape of every shingle on the roof of the old house opposite," she told her diary bitterly. Charles Tupper, who was a doctor as well as the Premier of Nova Scotia, came to check on her health every day. John A. Macdonald sent get-well wishes. Soon Mercy had a collection of the statesmen's visiting cards, each with a photograph. (Photography was still a new and thrilling process.) "The gentlemen have all been having their likenesses taken," she wrote. "Papa's is only tolerable."

At last she was well enough to dine downstairs, and she sat beside John A. Macdonald. "What an old humbug he is," she wrote mischievously in her diary that night. But she liked him better than George Brown, who did not dance and never knew what to say to young ladies.

Brown had too much on his mind for chit-chat, but behind closed doors he had a lot to say. Each day the thirty-three delegates – from Canada East and West, New Brunswick, Nova Scotia, Prince Edward Island, and Newfoundland – met to plan the new nation. They made speeches and posed questions. Sometimes they shouted and pounded the table. They argued over which powers should be given to the national government and which to the provinces. They planned a House of Commons and a Senate. They debated how to protect minorities. They agreed to build a railway from Halifax to Quebec.

After drafting the details of Confederation at Quebec in 1864, the Fathers of Confederation travelled to Montreal and Toronto – and to Niagara Falls

They even looked ahead to the day when the new nation would expand west across the plains to British Columbia.

The delegates wrote out seventy-two resolutions which were to be the foundation for the new nation. George Brown scribbled a happy note to his wife in Toronto: "All right! Constitution adopted – a most creditable document. Is it not wonderful?" The delegates and their families began a triumphal tour through the Canadas, and Mercy Ann Coles finally got to wear her blue silk gown. She even went to Niagara Falls, and was speechless with admiration.

Before the end of 1864, barely five months after George Brown's amazing proposal, it seemed that Confederation was almost a reality. But many obstacles lay ahead. George Coles, Mercy Ann's father, would help to create some of them.

The Battle for Confederation

There would be no Confederation in 1865, or in 1866 either. George Coles did not support the seventy-two resolutions, and he went home to Prince Edward Island to fight them. The plan might be good for Canada East and

Canada West, he had decided, but the Maritime colonies would be dwarfed and left powerless. William Henry Pope fought for Confederation, but most Prince Edward Islanders shared George Coles's feelings, and they made him premier. Soon the idea of Confederation was near death throughout Atlantic Canada. The excitement of Charlottetown was gone, and Maritimers were asking why they should be pulled into Confederation just to solve the problems of Canada East and Canada West. When New Brunswick held an election, the supporters of Confederation were driven from office.

Ambrose Shea and Frederick Carter had gone to the Quebec Conference on behalf of the colony of Newfoundland. Both men liked the Confederation plan, and they went home to urge Newfoundlanders to join Canada. However, most Newfoundlanders had always felt closer to Britain than to North America. Canada seemed remote and foreign and threatening. "Your sons will all be conscripted into Canada's armies and sent to leave their bones in the deserts of the west," cried one opponent.

Frederick Carter, who was the Premier of Newfoundland, decided the people must make the final decision. The election was furiously fought, but Newfoundland's choice was clear. The islanders rejected Confederation.

Robert Harris's painting of the Fathers of Confederation at Quebec was lost when the Parliament Buildings in Ottawa burned down in 1916. Artist Rex Woods painted this re-creation of it.

When photography was new, William Notman of Montreal was Canada's greatest photographer, and he took pictures of many famous people. This is George-Etienne Cartier, who led Quebec into Confederation.

"We are sold for the price of a sheepskin," thundered Joseph Howe in Halifax when he learned that the seventy-two resolutions (written on sheepskin parchment) included Canada's offer to pay some of Nova Scotia's debts. Nova Scotia's great statesman did not want his beloved colony to become one small part of Canada. Some Nova Scotians, including its premier, Charles Tupper, did argue in favour of Confederation and the railway to the Canadas it would bring. But so many Nova Scotians opposed the idea that Dr. Tupper did not dare call a vote on Confederation.

In Canada East, George-Etienne Cartier, leader of the Bleu party, led the fight for Confederation. In 1837, Cartier had been a Patriote rebel at St-Denis, but later he grew to admire the British empire so much that he said a French Canadian was an Englishman who spoke French! Cartier and other French-Canadian leaders were confident that Confederation would serve French Canada well. Twenty years earlier, they had defeated Lord Durham's plans to swallow up the French, and now they were playing important roles in shaping the new nation. French Canadians would have their own province, Quebec, and they would share a vast country with English Canada. Cartier had a powerful personality and a beautiful speaking voice. His arguments for Confederation did much to win French Canada's support.

In Canada West, Confederation was popular. Canada West would become a province named Ontario, instead of being yoked together with Canada East. It already had more people than any other colony in British North America, and Confederation appealed to its ambitions. And the old rivals, John A. Macdonald and George Brown, made an unstoppable team in their home province – although working together for Confederation had not made them friends.

Slowly the tide turned in some of the Maritime colonies. Prince Edward Island and Newfoundland held to their refusal to join Confederation, but in 1866, supporters of Confederation returned to power in New Brunswick.

The battle was fiercest in Nova Scotia. Arguments flared in every household from Yarmouth to Sydney. Joseph Howe

The fashion of pressing suits and pant legs smooth and flat came in after Confederation. But Joseph Howe, the great orator, politician, and newspaperman of Nova Scotia, would probably have been rough-edged and rumpled in any age.

inspired the "antis"; the proposal should not be called Confederation but "Botheration," he wrote scornfully. When Nova Scotia newspaperman Jonathan McCully came home from Quebec to argue for Confederation, the owner of his newspaper fired him. McCully had to start a new paper, while in his old one Howe tore the Confederation idea to shreds.

If Nova Scotia had held an election, the opponents of Confederation would surely have won. But the British government wanted Nova Scotia to agree, and at last the wily premier, Charles Tupper, devised a plan. He suggested that the Nova Scotia Assembly should vote in favour of the general idea of Confederation, then attend another conference that might produce better terms than the ones settled on at Quebec. The debate in the Assembly raged late into the night, but when the vote was held, Tupper and his supporters won. It was done "at black midnight," Joseph Howe said furiously.

Late in 1866, delegates from Canada East, Canada West, New Brunswick, and Nova Scotia sailed to London, England, to work out the last details of the Confederation plan. At the Westminster Conference, John A. Macdonald emerged as the star of Confederation. He was a master political fixer – as well as being a man of vision. He could charm almost anyone, and even George Brown admitted that his old enemy was "steady as a rock." With Cartier's help, Macdonald guided Confederation through every crisis. As Britain's Parliament prepared to pass the British North America Act, creating the new nation, the delegates agreed that John A. would be its first prime minister.

But what would the nation be called? The delegates settled on "Canada" – although people had proposed "Acadia," "British North America," and even "Hochelaga." Leonard Tilley, the Premier of New Brunswick, looked in his Bible and found a psalm that read, "He shall have dominion from sea to sea and from the river to the ends of the earth." The Dominion of Canada was born.

July 1, 1867, was a Monday. The weather was fine across the new nation. At dawn, the cannon of every fort

Creating Canada

The British North America Act made Canada a "federation" in 1867. There was a government in Ottawa for the whole country, but there was also a government in each province to administer local affairs. The problem in a federation is: who runs what?

John A. Macdonald wanted to keep as much power in Ottawa as possible. He wanted the provinces kept under Ottawa's control. The BNA Act listed certain things the provinces could do – and all the powers that were left over belonged to Ottawa. But John A. could not keep all these powers in his hands for ever. Soon the provinces would gain more rights and powers, and become equal partners in Confederation.

The Fathers of Confederation created the House of Commons. Everyone who could vote could help choose the members of Parliament who sat in the House of Commons. Every part of the country had members of Parliament – how many depending on its population. The leader of the party with the most members of Parliament became prime minister.

The Fathers of Confederation also created the Senate. Senators were appointed by the prime minister, not elected by the people. John A. Macdonald believed the Senate should restrain the House of Commons. He wanted to make sure that ordinary people did not have too much say in running the country. Each region (not each province) had the same number of senators.

The governor general still had a lot of influence over how Canada was governed in 1867. The governor general represented the British government as well as the queen. Because Canadians respected and honoured the queen's representative, he was able to disagree with Canadian leaders. Over the years, governors general gradually agreed to leave decisions to the Senate and the House of Commons, but it would be many decades before a Canadian became governor general.

In 1869, Newfoundland fought an election to decide whether or not to join Confederation. "Come near at your peril, Canadian wolf," sang the "antis." Their leader, Charles Fox Bennett, claimed that Newfoundlanders would be taken into Canada's army and would "leave their bones in the deserts of the west." Newfoundland elected him as premier, and it was eighty more years before Newfoundland joined Canada.

and naval ship roared out salutes. Religious services were held and parades began in hundreds of towns. Brass bands, militia companies, and local clubs marched proudly through Halifax, Saint John, Ste-Hyacinthe, and Sarnia. In Kingston they played cricket, in Barrie they had sailing competitions, in Dunnville there was horse racing. Homes were decorated with bunting and flowers. Bonfires blazed, fireworks exploded, picnics were organized, and speeches were given in honour of Confederation.

Not everyone was ready to celebrate. Diehard opponents of Confederation hung out black wreaths. Young Quebecker Wilfrid Laurier denounced Confederation as a threat to French Canada. (He would change his mind one day and go on to become prime minister.) Joseph Howe was still opposed to Confederation in 1867, but later he would join John A.'s government, still fighting for better terms for Nova Scotia. Newfoundland would not join Confederation until 1949, but in 1873 Prince Edward

Thomas D'Arcy McGee

Irish immigrants had been coming to Canada for decades. Some were prosperous farmers and merchants. Others were starving refugees who staggered from the immigrant ships after Ireland's terrible Potato Famine of 1848. And a few had to flee Ireland after fighting against British rule there. Thomas D'Arcy McGee was one of these. But after he settled in Montreal, McGee decided Canada could be a good home for the Catholic Irish. He became their spokesman, and they elected him to Parliament in Ottawa.

A politician, journalist, and poet, McGee dreamed of a Canadian nation where Protestant and Catholic, French, Irish, English, and all others could share a proud new country. "I see in the not remote distance, one great nationality bound by the blue rim of ocean," he cried, and he became the prophet of a Canadian nation under Confederation.

McGee's silvery words swayed many to the cause of Confederation. But the Fenians hated him. The Fenians were Irishmen who fought for rebellion against Britain, and they attacked Canada as a way to attack Britain. But D'Arcy McGee rallied Irish Canadians against the Fenians, and they found little support here. Canada drove back the small bands of Fenians who made several raids from the United States in 1866.

Less than a year after Confederation, as McGee walked to his boarding-house after a late-night session in Parliament, a gunman put a pistol to his head and shot him. McGee fell dead on the wooden sidewalk of Sparks Street. Pat Whelan, a Fenian, was tried and convicted for the murder of Confederation's first martyr. Whelan protested his innocence to the last, but he was hanged on Nicholas Street in Ottawa – the last man to be publicly hanged in Canada.

Island agreed to become a province, and Mercy Ann Coles became a Canadian at last.

In the streets of Toronto, people sang and let off firecrackers on the eve of that first Dominion Day. George Brown sat all night at his desk in the office of *The Globe.* He had left politics more than a year before, confident that, with Confederation coming, his work in politics was done. Now he was writing the whole Confederation story for his newspaper. "We hail the birthday of a new nationality," he finished triumphantly, just as dawn broke.

In Ottawa, Governor General Lord Monck swore in the Cabinet ministers of the first government of Canada. Then the governor general and the prime minister, who had been knighted by Queen Victoria and was now Sir John A. Macdonald, went out together to review the troops and greet the cheering crowds.

Into the West

The makers of Confederation intended to extend Canada from sea to sea. Ontario's farmers wanted the new country to include the vast western prairie; if Canada did not move west, the Americans might move in, and Canada would be unable to grow. Barely a year after Confederation, George-Etienne Cartier went to London on behalf of Canada and arranged for the new nation to buy the rights to Rupert's Land, the vast fur-trading territory which the Hudson's Bay Company had held since 1670. In 1869, William McDougall set out for Red River to become the first lieutenant-governor of Canada's Northwest Territories,

Louis Riel (centre) *sits among the members of the Manitoba Provisional Government he formed in 1869. When British and Canadian forces arrived in 1870, its leaders had to flee across the border.*

English-speaking Canada was shocked by the news that Louis Riel's Métis government at Red River had executed Thomas Scott, a young troublemaker from Ontario. This engraving, which appeared in the Canadian Illustrated News*, shows the execution as a cold-blooded murder. The picture probably helped to make readers even more determined to avenge Scott and destroy Riel.*

which in those days meant the old Hudson's Bay territory.

McDougall never reached his destination. The Métis of Red River had not been consulted in the negotiations over Rupert's Land, but they did not intend their land to be overrun by governors from Ottawa and settlers from Ontario. Louis Riel and the newly formed Red River Council took charge. Métis horsemen galloped down from Red River to Pembina to stop McDougall before he could enter Métis territory. Next they seized the Hudson's Bay Company's Fort Garry, in the heart of the Red River country. The council declared it wanted to negotiate with Canada on behalf of all the people of Red River, and it won the support of many of the English-speaking "mixed-blood" settlers of Red River.

Riel was twenty-five years old, a dark, stocky man with a thick black beard. He had returned from school in Montreal with a passion to lead his people. He sent the demands of the Red River Council to Ottawa. Red River must enter Confederation as a province, the council declared. The settlers must be consulted, and the rights of the Métis to their language and religion must be guaranteed.

Riel's decisive actions forced Prime Minister Macdonald to halt the Canadian takeover of Red River. Soon he agreed that Red River would enter Confederation as a province, not as a territory to be run from Ottawa. The Métis seemed to have won. But in Red River, a handful of English-speaking, Protestant settlers from Ontario refused to accept the rule of the French-speaking, Catholic Métis. They defied the Red River Council and fought Riel's authority. Riel had one of them, young Thomas Scott, shot by a firing squad.

Hunters with rifles killed thousands of buffalo for their pelts, or simply for sport, leaving the bones to litter the prairie. For years after the herds had been destroyed, buffalo bones were loaded into boxcars and hauled east to be made into fertilizer.

Ontario erupted in fury when Scott was executed, and the government of Canada decided to send troops to take control of Red River. While the soldiers struggled on the long trek across what is now northern Ontario by boat and canoe, Louis Riel fled south to the United States. Manitoba became a province of Canada on May 2, 1870 (exactly 200 years after the founding of the Hudson's Bay Company), and half a million hectares of land were promised to the Métis and their descendants. But instead of being saluted as a maker of Confederation, Riel was an exile.

The Métis of Red River were not the only people Canada had to deal with when it tried to take over the lands where the Hudson's Bay Company had traded. In the early 1870s, the great Cree, Assiniboine, and Blackfoot confederacies still commanded the plains. With the buffalo herds being hunted almost to extinction, the tribes were hungry, but the land was still theirs. If Canada wanted the West, Canada would have to talk to them. During the 1870s, Canadian officials talked.

The government's Indian agents sat under the hot sun and the broad sky with the tribes, bands, and nations of the plains. Canada intended to take most of the land, but Native leaders resisted. The Cree chief Pitikwahanapiwiyan,

The Man Who Saved the Buffalo

Michel Pablo's ancestors had been buffalo hunters for ten thousand years. But in the 1880s, rifles, railways, and relentless slaughter destroyed North America's buffalo herds. All over the plains, the buffalo-hunting nations fell from greatness to poverty in barely a decade.

Michel Pablo lived on the Flathead reserve in Montana. He rounded up a few buffalo calves and kept them on the reserve. By the early 1900s, he had the largest herd in the world. But Michel Pablo's people lost their reserve to settlers in 1906. There would be no room left for the wild buffalo.

At that time, Canada was creating national parks in the West, and the Canadian government offered to buy Michel Pablo's herd – if he would drive them to Buffalo National Park, near Wainwright, Alberta. Pablo agreed to do the job for $250 a head, and the great buffalo drive was on.

They called it "the longest, costliest, most frustrating roundup ever." In the heat and dust of an Alberta summer, Native cowboys drove 400 buffalo north from Montana. The drive brought a great animal back from the edge of extinction. Today, descendants of Michel Pablo's herd make up roughly half of all the buffalo in the world. They roam wild in Wood Buffalo National Park, in northern Alberta.

The dignity and wisdom of Crowfoot, seen here with his family in 1884, were admired by all who dealt with him, but rarely captured by photographers. Crowfoot was widely mourned when he died.

called Poundmaker, said, "This is our land. It is not a piece of pemmican to be cut off and given in little pieces back to us." Another Cree, Piapot, was against making treaties. He did not trust the government's agents, even though the Canadians claimed to give their word "for as long as the rivers ran, as long as the grass grew, as long as men walked on two legs."

The government was determined to get its way. Government agents bullied, threatened, and offered money, and one by one most of the chiefs gave in. They felt they had to. "If left to ourselves we are gone," declared Isapo-muxika, or Crowfoot, who was chief of the Blackfoot. Smallpox had ravaged his people, settlers were coming from the west and the south, and the buffalo herds were all but gone. He hoped that, if they signed the treaties, his people would get help to settle down and turn from hunting to farming. The treaties promised that kind of help, so in September 1877 Crowfoot signed a treaty at Blackfoot Crossing on the Bow River and led his people to a reserve near Calgary. Most of the other prairie nations signed treaties. The great prairie West was becoming part of settled Canada.

Policing the plains became the job of the North-West Mounted Police. In midsummer 1874, the new force rode out of Dufferin, Manitoba, and headed west, 300 strong, with their wagon train stretched out behind them. They looked like an army, dressed in their scarlet tunics and tall white helmets. Even their horses matched – greys for one company, blacks for the next. That summer the Mounted Police crossed 1500 kilometres of hot, dry plain. Men and horses were staggering and weak before they reached the safety of the foothills of the Rockies, where water and fodder were plentiful. Yet the American whisky traders of "Whoop-Up Country" (as the territory north of Montana was called), who had been selling illegal whisky to the Native people, fled before them. Canadian law had come to the Canadian plains.

To keep order across Canada's vast new territories seemed an impossible task for 300 Mounted Police. But the Mounties earned the respect of angry Native bands and land-hungry settlers alike. Ta-tanka I-yotank, called Sitting Bull, and 5000 Sioux crossed the border in 1877, with the

In their early years in the West, Mountie patrols not only caught the criminals and tried them, they also did all kinds of small jobs. In this picture, a Mountie delivers mail to a homesick settler from Ontario.

Massacre in the Cypress Hills

The Cypress Hills rise only a few hundred metres above the dry prairie of what is now southern Alberta and Saskatchewan, but that is enough to make them the highest ground between the Rockies and Labrador. Wolves and deer, hunters and whisky traders were all drawn to their forested slopes.

In 1872, an Assiniboine band built its winter lodges in the Cypress Hills. The Assiniboine had just made peace with the Blackfoot Confederacy. Now that the fighting was over, they hoped for prosperous hunting in the hills. Instead, they found American hunters spreading poison to kill wolves for their pelts, and American traders offering the poison of liquor to the Native bands. Both hunters and traders moved back and forth across the unmarked border, evading the law on both sides, and they were well armed. They disrupted the Assiniboine people's own hunting, but no one could control them.

In May 1873, after the whisky traders and the Natives quarrelled over horses, the traders attacked the Assiniboine lodges. Thirty-six Natives were shot down in the raid, and the traders burned the village.

News of the Cypress Hills Massacre helped to convince the government in Ottawa that it needed a police force to keep order in the new prairie territories, and so the North-West Mounted Police was created. When the Mounties marched in, outlaw traders retreated from Canada. Although the killings in the Cypress Hills went unpunished, they were not repeated across the plains.

United States Cavalry not far behind. South of the border the Sioux had been at war, but Inspector James Walsh met them with just a handful of Mounties. He promised that if they kept the peace while they were in Canada there would be no trouble. The Sioux stayed in Canada for four years, and the American soldiers stayed out.

The Mounted Police helped to keep the peace, but Canada paid little attention to the promises it had made to the Native nations in the treaties it had forced them to sign. In 1876 Parliament passed the Indian Act. Canada's Indian agents took control of the reserves, and Native children began to be sent away to school, so they would not learn Native ways. Canada wanted to turn the Native peoples into ordinary Canadians as quickly as it could. It wanted them to give up their languages, their beliefs, and their treaty rights as free people. Few Native people wanted to do that. They resisted, but it would be a long time before they began to recover the power and the freedom they had once had.

The Whole Nation Minus One

On the Pacific coast, British Columbians were watching as the new nation marched west. In 1870, British Columbia sent delegates east to talk to the Canadian government about joining Confederation. British Columbia was a long way from Ottawa, they pointed out, and a long way even from Manitoba. British Columbians were independent-minded people who had not ruled out joining the United States, which was closer to them than Canada. If they were to join Confederation, they declared, Canada would have to build a road across the Prairies and the mountains to the Pacific. A railway would have to follow later.

George-Etienne Cartier, who was acting prime minister because Macdonald was ill, scorned this talk of roads. Join Confederation, he promised exuberantly, and we will build a railway to the Pacific in ten years. The delighted British Columbians could hardly believe their ears. They shook

"WE IN CANADA SEEM TO HAVE LOST ALL IDEA OF JUSTICE, HONOR AND INTEGRITY."—THE MAIL, 26TH SEPTEMBER.

J.W. Bengough was Canada's most successful cartoonist in the years after Confederation. His favourite target was Sir John A. Macdonald, here seen at the time of his resignation, talking to Opposition leader Alexander Mackenzie.

hands with the Canadians, and British Columbia became the sixth province of Canada in 1871.

Two years later, the American-Canadian International Boundary Commission completed the survey that marked out the border between Canada and the United States. That same year, 1873, James Pope (William Henry Pope's brother) led Prince Edward Island into Confederation as Canada's seventh province. Since 1870 the plains west of Manitoba had been Canadian territories, although Alberta and Saskatchewan did not become provinces until 1905. In 1880, Canada acquired the Arctic Islands from Britain. Even though most of the North was still unknown to all but the Inuit, no one consulted them about this transfer.

Newfoundland still had not joined Confederation, but, from the Atlantic to the Pacific to the Arctic, the territory of the Dominion of Canada now truly stretched from sea to sea to sea. It was time for the railway to pull it together.

The Great Railway

Ten years after George-Etienne Cartier's rash promise, work on the railway had barely begun. During the election of 1872, Sir John A. accepted money from the "railway barons," businessmen who wanted the contract to build the new line. When he was found out, he had to resign in disgrace. The second Prime Minister of Canada, Alexander Mackenzie, called the railway to the Pacific "an act of insane recklessness." It looked as if he was right.

The Canadian Pacific Railway was the most ambitious railway project in the world. It was going to cost a fortune. Tracks had to be pushed through the rock and muskeg of northern Ontario, across the prairie, and through the mountains. No one even knew if passes suitable for railway lines existed in British Columbia's mountain ranges. For years, surveyors had scrambled up and down the slopes and valleys in search of a route. The obstacles seemed insurmountable.

About 15 000 Chinese workers, nearly all men, came to work on the British Columbia section of the Canadian Pacific Railway. The work was gruelling and dangerous, and many died.

The Mennonite Pioneers

Mennonites began coming to Canada from the United States soon after the American Revolution. Their religion forbade them to fight or to serve in armies, and they came seeking a homeland where their young men would not have to be soldiers. Canada's first Mennonite communities grew up along the Grand River of southern Ontario in the late 1700s.

Almost a hundred years later, Canada wanted immigrants to settle in its new province of Manitoba. Mennonite Jacob Shantz of Berlin, Ontario, visited Manitoba. He thought it would make a good home for his Mennonite brethren of southern Russia. In 1874, Russian Mennonites travelled by boat, train, and oxcart to Manitoba.

Soon almost 7000 more Mennonites came from Russia to join them. In a few decades, there were prosperous Mennonite communities across the West.

Then an American "railway general" called William Van Horne became manager of the Canadian Pacific Railway. Van Horne said he liked things "big and bulgy like myself," and the CPR was the kind of challenge he loved. Soon he had his work crews racing west over the Prairies and conquering the "bottomless bogs" of northern Ontario. By then the surveyors had found a route through the mountains, and workers began fighting inch by inch into British Columbia's rugged terrain. "Fix it up," Van Horne would cry whenever a problem slowed the pace of construction. "Fix it up!"

Thousands of men laboured to build the Canadian Pacific Railway. There were Canadians, Americans, Germans, Swedes, Finns, and Italians laying track. Six thousand workers came from China to drive the line east through the canyons and passes of British Columbia towards the work crews moving west from the plains. Rock falls, dynamite explosions, winter cold, and summer heat took hundreds of lives, but the work went on.

In 1885, the railway was nearly completed – and nearly bankrupt. The costs were enormous and the debts mountainous. Van Horne's cashbox was empty. Then a new rebellion flared suddenly on the Prairies – and the railway was in the middle of it.

Canada had never fulfilled its promises to the Métis of the Northwest, and new settlers were taking the land. The Métis turned to Louis Riel again. He returned from exile, older now and more bitter (some claimed he was insane), and more than ever determined to lead his people. When he raised the Métis flag at Batoche in 1885, the North-West Rebellion was under way. The Mounted Police marched a hundred men to the Métis camp at Duck Lake. Métis general Gabriel Dumont and his men sent them flying in retreat, and soon the Mounties abandoned their base at Fort Carleton. The Métis fighters had won every skirmish.

The Native nations might have joined the Métis, for few of them were content. Those who had signed treaties were poor and hungry, and Canada was not giving them the help it had promised. Plains Cree bands led by Big Bear and Poundmaker still resisted the treaties, and Riel urged them to join him. Some bitter and angry young warriors led raids and ambushes when the Métis began to fight. But the chiefs were skilled war leaders and they could see the power that Canada now had. They urged their people to stay out of the conflict.

John A. Macdonald, who had been back in office since 1878, moved to smash the rising, and the new railway was there to help. Within a few days, troops were boarding trains in Ottawa and Toronto. A few days more, and they were on the plains and marching out to fight. Despite the

When the Mounties sleighed into Duck Lake early in 1885 to control the rebellious Métis, Gabriel Dumont and his men easily defeated them. Twelve Mounties and volunteers were killed. If Louis Riel had not held back Dumont's men, few of the rest would have escaped.

C.P.R. 148

Photographing the Last Spike

The photographer sets up the most famous photograph in Canadian history – the driving of the last spike at Craigellachie, B.C., on November 7, 1885. Young Edward Mallandaine peers from behind Donald Smith, who raises his hammer. In the background, William Van Horne's young son shouts out in excitement.

Despite the skill of the Métis cavalry, Riel's rebellion was doomed once the new railway rushed troops to the plains. The last battle was fought at Batoche in Saskatchewan, on May 12, 1885.

Pitikwahanapiwiyan, called Poundmaker, did not want to join Louis Riel's rebellion, but many of the young Cree did. After Riel's defeat, Poundmaker decided to surrender. "You did not catch me," he told General Middleton. "You have got me because I wanted justice."

skill and courage of Gabriel Dumont's Métis fighters, the Canadian troops overwhelmed the rising. Dumont fled to the United States, but Louis Riel was captured and put on trial. In November 1885 he was hanged in Regina. Big Bear and Poundmaker were thrown in jail, even though only a handful of their young men had gone to war – and against their urging, at that.

As a reward for its help during the North-West Rebellion, the Canadian Pacific Railway got the money it

When the prime minister and his wife rode the CPR in 1886, Agnes Macdonald decided the front of the locomotive was the best place from which to see the Rockies. Sir John preferred the comfortable passenger cars. Soon, riding the cowcatcher became a fad, and CPR photographs like this one helped promote it.

needed, and construction workers closed the last gaps in the railway line. The tracks from east and west met in the British Columbia mountains, and William Van Horne rode west to see the last spike driven at Craigellachie. He insisted on a plain iron spike just like all the others. "All I can say is that the work has been well done in every way," he said when the spike was hammered into place. "All aboard for the Pacific," cried the conductor.

In barely twenty years, the Dominion of Canada had been dreamed of, begun, and almost completed. Great deeds had been accomplished, great hardships endured, great injustices suffered. Many complained or grumbled about Confederation, and they had cause, but a new nation had been created.

In 1886, John A. Macdonald and his wife rode the great railway to the Pacific. Agnes Macdonald was determined to see every spectacular view of the mountains. She had a chair mounted on the cowcatcher at the front of the locomotive, and there she sat. Back in a comfortable coach, John A. had much to be proud of as the train puffed on towards the booming new railway town called Vancouver. His friends had said that he would be in heaven looking down by the time the CPR was completed. His enemies had predicted that he would be looking up from hell. "Now I am taking the horizontal view," joked the man who had once described his goal as "one people, great in territory, great in resources, great in enterprise."

This poster announced the opening of the Canadian Pacific Railway to passengers travelling from coast to coast.

Chapter 4

Sunny Ways

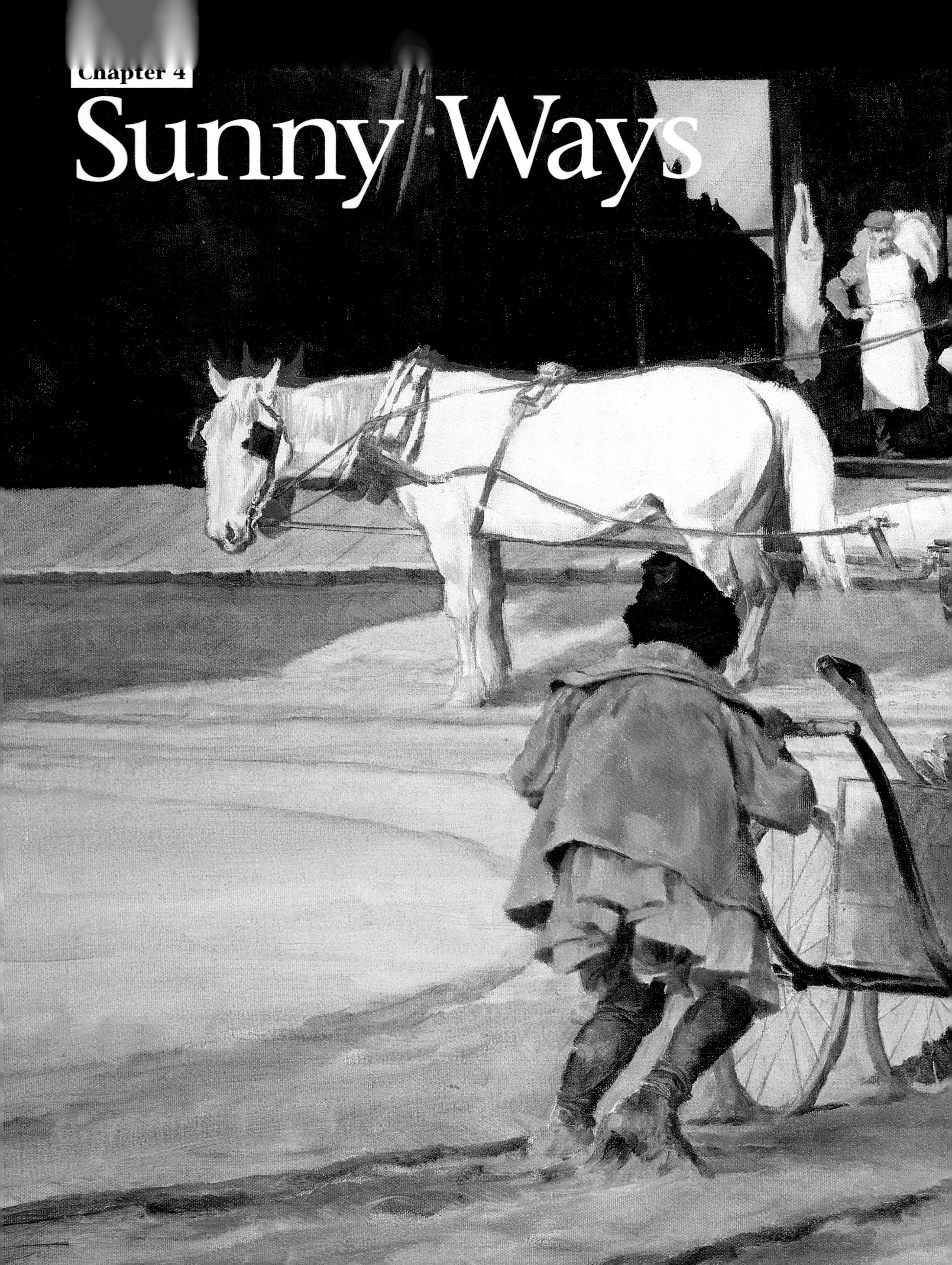

MARKET.
H.FER

WILFRID LAURIER STROLLED DOWN THE STEPS OF PARLIAMENT IN Ottawa. In his days as a young lawyer and newspaper editor, he had written passionate articles against Confederation. Now, in 1896, he was leader of the Liberal Party in Parliament, and he was as committed to Confederation as John A. Macdonald had been. He was the first French Canadian to lead one of Canada's national political parties, and as leader of the Opposition he was just one step from being prime minister. He was considered the best-dressed man in Ottawa, and everyone agreed that he was charming and graceful. But what kind of leader was he? people wanted to know. Where did he stand on the great issues of the day?

Always elegant, well-dressed, and charming, Wilfrid Laurier seemed unbeatable on the campaign trail from 1896 until 1911. That year, opposition to his plan for free trade with the United States drove him from office.

Previous pages:
Despite the rough, muddy roads, a brand-new Stanley Steamer makes a wonderful toy for a well-to-do family. Meanwhile, most people still make do with a horse and wagon, and children from poor families still gather coal along the railway tracks.

In 1896, Canada seemed to be adrift. Macdonald, "the old chieftain," had died in 1891. In the five years that had followed, Canada had had four prime ministers, but no real leader had come forth to fill the shoes of Sir John A. In Ottawa, politicians argued with each other and fought with the provincial leaders. Across the country, people seemed unable to settle their differences. There was tension and distrust between the French and the English, and between East and West.

The Manitoba Schools Question was the great issue of the day, and it drew angry words from all sides. Manitoba's French-speaking Catholic children had had their own schools until 1890. Then the government of Manitoba had stopped paying for them. It said the French-speaking population had become so small that the schools were no longer needed. French Canadians were furious over the loss of their rights.

Everything the Conservative prime ministers tried to do only seemed to make things worse. As an election campaign loomed, someone challenged Wilfrid Laurier: how would he and his Liberals solve this terrible problem when everyone else had failed?

Laurier replied with one of Aesop's fables, a story he had learned as a child in St-Lin, Quebec. In this fable, the sun and the wind made a bet to see who could get the coat off a man's back. The wind howled and shrieked around

A one-room school in Ontario's Muskoka District in 1887. The children vary widely in age.

the man, but the harder it blew, the more tightly he clutched his coat around him. Then it was the sun's turn. With a warm smile, the sun beamed upon the man, and soon he was so warm that he pulled off his coat himself. There had been enough windy threats about the Manitoba Schools Question, Laurier said. If he were prime minister, he would try the sunny way.

It seemed like a reassuring answer, and in mid-summer of 1896 Wilfrid Laurier became prime minister. The man of the sunny ways would be Canada's leader for fifteen years. His times were not sunny for everyone, of course. There were neither health-care plans nor unemployment insurance for workers. Punishments were harsh, even for children, and prisons were hellish places. But for many Canadians, Laurier's years brought good times and prosperity. The gold horseshoe tiepin he liked to wear for good luck seemed to promise a bright future for a growing country.

A wedding in Dartmouth, Nova Scotia, in the late 1800s. In Victorian times, formal behaviour spread from the rich and powerful to the middle and working classes. Top hats, canes, and elaborate lace dresses became the proper attire for weddings.

In 1897, Laurier and his wife, Zoë, went to London, England, for Queen Victoria's Diamond Jubilee, a celebration of her sixty years on the throne. The British empire was at its peak of might and power, and the Jubilee brought together imperial leaders from India, Africa, Australia, and all the rest of Britain's empire. None shone brighter than Laurier, who became Sir Wilfrid when the aged queen knighted her Canadian prime minister.

Gold Fever

During the same summer that Wilfrid Laurier became prime minister, George Carmack and his Native brothers-in-law, Skookum Jim and Tagish Charlie, went prospecting for gold in the Klondike River Valley of the Yukon country. A fellow prospector had said they should try Rabbit Creek, so they headed that way. There, on August 17, 1896, they found gold "lying thick between the flaky slabs of rock like cheese in a sandwich." Rabbit Creek has been called Bonanza Creek ever since. It took nearly a year for the news to get out, but then stories about "a ton of gold" flashed around the world by telegraph.

Every miner heading for the Yukon had to take a year's worth of goods with him. To cross the Chilkoot Pass, a miner had to go up and down that steep slope many times, until his whole stock was at the other side.

Officers of the North-West Mounted Police keep law and order during Canada's first gold rush, on the Yukon River near Dawson, in 1898.

In Canada, the United States, Europe, and Australia, 100000 people (mostly men) dropped what they were doing and headed for Bonanza Creek. Some went to Edmonton and spent months struggling overland to the North. Most sailed to Skagway, Alaska, and took "The Trail of '98." First they hiked over the White Pass or the fearsome Chilkoot Pass. At the foot of the thousand-metre Chilkoot, Mounties would let them go on only if they had a year's supplies with them. Gold-seekers struggled up and down the snow steps of the pass, bent double under load after load, until all their precious supplies were across. If they made it, they built rafts and floated down the Yukon River to the goldfields.

Where the Klondike flows into the Yukon River, Dawson City was born. Hotelkeepers, storekeepers, clerks, gamblers, entertainers, and prospectors poured in from all over the globe. In a month, Dawson became the largest Canadian city west of Winnipeg, and it was bursting with people frantic to get rich. A few did, for at least fifty million dollars' worth of gold came out of the Klondike. But the miners spent about as much as they found, and many left poorer than when they arrived. A young bank clerk named Robert Service got rich by writing about the miners. His poems about "the strange things done in the midnight sun, by the men who moil for gold" made him famous and popular all over the world.

The Yukon was a rough, wild place during the gold rush, but it was not lawless. Canada created a special military unit, the Yukon Field Force, to protect the border and discourage the many American prospectors from trying to add the Yukon to the United States. Meanwhile, the Mounties kept order among the miners. Because of the gold rush, the Yukon became a territory of Canada, with Dawson its first capital. In a couple of years there was a railway to carry miners over White Pass, and paddle-wheelers, rather than rafts, took them down the Yukon to the goldfields. But by then the Klondike boom was already fading.

Naturalist Martha Louise Munger left fashionable society in Chicago in 1898 to join the Klondike gold rush. There she married George Black, commissioner of the Yukon Territory. She was seventy when her husband retired from the House of Commons in 1935, but she campaigned for and won his seat, becoming the second woman ever elected to the Canadian Parliament.

The Last Best West

"The twentieth century will belong to Canada," said Wilfrid Laurier boldly in 1904. All the country needed was people, and more people were coming to Canada than ever before. To bring jobs to Canada, John A. Macdonald had created the National Policy, and Laurier maintained that policy. Under the National Policy, Canada collected fees (called tariffs) on foreign goods coming to Canada. The fees made imported goods more costly, and farmers complained about the high prices they paid. But enterprising Canadians became manufacturers, and American businessmen came here to build "branch plants." The factories made work for Canadians, and also for the immigrants who came to join them. Laurier predicted that Canada's six million people would soon be sixty million.

Hundreds of thousands of settlers also headed for the prairie West so recently claimed from the Native nations. At first, the most successful were not farmers but ranchers. As soon as the railway opened, cattle barons began stocking the southwestern Alberta plains with beef cattle. Grizzled cowpunchers, with only a saddle, a rifle, and a Navajo blanket to their names, guided the herds from the dry shortgrass prairie to winter shelter in the Rocky Mountain foothills. Canadian Pacific trains and ships hauled the "beef bonanza" away to market in Chicago and London.

Immigrants from eastern Canada, the United States, Britain, and Europe began to stream into the Canadian plains, drawn by advertisements which called the region "the last best west" – the last part of North America that was not yet crowded with farms and towns. In 1913, Canada welcomed over 400000 immigrants – more than in any single year before or since. Most of them were heading for the Prairies.

Isaac Barr, an English clergyman, led 2000 English settlers to Saskatchewan. Barr wanted to create a little corner of England on the plains, but his followers were city folk, not farmers. Barr had no idea how to organize or lead them, and the Barr colonists' first years were desperate ones. Thousands more immigrants came in family groups or on their own, as did the "remittance men." These were young men whose wealthy families shipped them off and "remitted" money to them so long as they stayed away. Remittance men were famous on the Prairies for lounging about and organizing foxhunts, but almost never for breaking the tough prairie sod.

Many Ontario farmers went west to find farmlands on the plains, but only a few French-speakers moved there.

Wheat and wildlife still seemed to be what Canada was known for when this truck was driving through Britain, urging immigration to Canada.

Despite Laurier's sunny ways, Manitoba had not reversed its decision to close its French-language schools. Although Manitoba, with its Métis traditions, had joined Confederation as a bilingual society, there were so many newcomers from Ontario, the United States, and Britain that English became the main language, not only in Manitoba but throughout the West.

Only a few Maritimers joined in the western migration. The age of sailing ships, of "wood, wind, and water," was ending, and the great Maritime sailing fleet had nearly vanished. For a while, it seemed that factories might bring new prosperity. Canada's first steelplant opened in Trenton, Nova Scotia, in 1883 and soon there was another one in Sydney, near the Cape Breton coalfields. But most of the new factories were built in central Canada, not the Maritimes. Maritimers began leaving their homes to look for work, but they went south to "the Boston states" more often than "up to Canada."

Canada had always preferred white, English-speaking immigrants. When the SS *Komagata Maru* tried to bring 400 East Indians to Vancouver in 1913, the passengers were prevented from landing, and Canada's first naval ship, HMCS *Rainbow*, helped drive them away again. But some Asians did reach Canada. Japanese settlers built up a thriving fishing fleet in Steveston, B.C., and Chinese immigrants continued to come in spite of the "head tax" they were obliged to pay.

In Eastern Europe, word of the last best west was spreading. Two Ukrainian farmers, Wasyl Eleniak and Ivan Pylypiw, settled in Alberta in 1891. They wrote home that Canada was a great country where farmers could find *vilni zemli* – free land – and live free from persecution. Slowly families from Poland and the empires of Russia and Austria set off for Canada and vilni zemli.

Many Canadians claimed that letting in settlers who were not British would create a "mongrel Canada." But Clifford Sifton, Laurier's Minister of Immigration, decided western Canada needed these farmers. "A stalwart peasant in a sheepskin coat, with a stout wife and a half-dozen

Poster for "Western Canada's Greatest Fair," which later became the Calgary Exhibition and Stampede. The first Stampede was held in 1912.

The Old Mill, *painted by Homer Watson in 1886. When Watson was a boy, his father was a miller on the Grand River in Canada West. Watson became one of the first important artists of Canada in the years after Confederation, and mills were among his favourite subjects.*

children, is good quality," said Sifton. (These were times when Canadian leaders felt comfortable describing people of non-British origin as if they were part of the livestock.) Sifton sent immigration agents to recruit farmers from Eastern Europe, and the flow became a torrent.

Whole communities that had suffered persecution or hardship began to move from Europe to the Prairies. In 1875, Icelanders had founded New Iceland around the community of Gimli ("Paradise") in Manitoba. The Doukhobours ("spirit wrestlers"), a religious sect from Russia, settled in Saskatchewan in 1898, but after disputes with their neighbours they trekked west to settle in the Kootenays of British Columbia. German-speaking Mennonites also came from Russia seeking religious freedom, and they settled in Manitoba and Saskatchewan. Many other European ethnic and religious groups settled in Canadian towns or founded their own communities.

In those days, Canada offered a quarter-section (160 acres, which is 65 hectares) of land to "homesteaders" who could pay ten dollars and who promised to live on the land and to build a house and barn on it within three years. The homesteaders "busted sod," ploughing under the tough cover of prairie grasses. In summer they had to endure 35°C heat, and they worried about drought and fire. For

Maryanne Caswell's Journey

"Amid waving of hankies and promises to write we left our pretty town, the only home we had ever known." Fourteen-year-old Maryanne Caswell wrote those words to her grandmother back in Ontario when the Caswells left to pioneer in the West in 1887.

"A long slow train . . . the seats and backs are wooden slats that can be pulled out, and the two facing and joining are used for a bed which mother used. Then, above, a large shelf is pulled down, and hangs by rods and hinges. This was our bed. . . . Then there is a room at the end of the car with a stove to cook on and water. At the other end are the washrooms."

The train trip from Toronto to Moose Jaw – a journey that had taken the old *voyageurs* three months by canoe – took the Caswells only three days. For another weary week they walked with the cows and sheep following along behind, to reach Saskatoon. "How tired we were of walk, walk!" wrote Maryanne. And when they finally arrived in Saskatoon there were only fourteen houses. "Where is the city?" Maryanne wanted to know. "On the map in the surveyor's office," was the answer.

safety from fast-moving grassfires, they had to plough a cleared circle around the homestead. In winter they put up with 40°-below cold and wild blizzards, with only the sod walls of their shanties for insulation. In a generation, the homesteaders turned the unbroken prairie grasslands into a sea of bright golden wheat fields that swayed like ocean waves in the prairie wind.

Imagine what it was like around 1905 for a Ukrainian girl new to western Canada. She had crossed the sea in the stinking hold of a steamship, crowded in with hundreds of others. In the new country, almost the only people who spoke her language were those who had travelled with her. After the long train journey from Montreal, the prairie made her heart sing: it looked like a fresh, new version of her old country. Perhaps her family had brought enough money to buy farm machinery, so her father did not have to go away to work on the railway or in the mines. Before the year was out, the family might have a real house to replace the sod shanty.

The girl walked down the concession road to the one-room school. She found, however, that the children called her stupid because she couldn't read English or even speak it very well. Some of them made fun of the clothes her mother made her, because they were different from theirs. However, the Ukrainian families had already begun their own church, and they were determined to have a school soon. They intended to preserve the Ukrainian language in this new land.

Meanwhile, what a relief to hurry home to the farmhouse. Mother would have good familiar borscht and perogies waiting, and Grandmother would be ready with stories about the old country. The family was glad to escape poverty and oppression in Europe, but in the safety and promise of the new land, the good memories could be cherished.

These prairie settlers were doing well. Instead of living in a sod hut, they had a solid house with an attic and a thatched roof.

Another family, with barely enough money for its fare, would not be so lucky. If the land agent considered them poor prospects, he would send them to poor land at the far end of his district. They might spend their first winter in a hut dug into the ground, with only planks for a roof. The father probably had to go away from home to find work, and big comforting meals would be few and far between.

Many families failed and were forced to move on to new districts or to the slums of cities. Enough remained, however, that in 1905 two new provinces, Alberta and Saskatchewan, were created.

What made it possible for these western settlements to grow so quickly? The railway. The train was as important to pioneering on the Prairies as the canoe had been in the fur trade. The big steam engines puffed through the forests, across the plains, and over the mountain passes, hauling long trains crowded with passengers, goods, and mail.

Marquis Wheat

It takes a special kind of wheat to produce good crops in western Canada's short summers and frigid winters. By 1903, the Central Experimental Farm in Ottawa had developed a strain of wheat tough enough for the prairie cold. It was called Marquis, and when it was ready to test, the scientists in Ottawa sent a sackful to a government farm in Indian Head, Saskatchewan.

When the boss, Angus Mackay, was ready to plant the wheat, he couldn't find it. He searched frantically. Finally he put a sign up in the barn, saying, "Please, whoever took the sackful of wheat marked Marquis for testing, return it at once. Urgent. No questions asked." The wheat came back – one of the men had taken it to feed his chickens! The Marquis wheat was planted and harvested and proved perfect for prairie farming, and its flour made good bread.

A few years later, an American railway offered a $1000 prize for the world's best wheat. The railway officials were expecting American wheat to win but, when a Saskatchewan farmer named Seager Wheeler took a sample of Marquis to the competition, he won the prize – and Marquis wheat became world-famous.

Trains brought the people to the land and took wheat, beef, or timber back to faraway customers.

Prairie towns grew up around the railway stations, and by the grain elevators where the wheat crop was weighed and stored until the boxcars arrived to haul it away. Soon there would be a church – with an Anglican steeple in a British-settled area, an onion-shaped dome in a Ukrainian one. There might be a Chinese restaurant and a Jewish family's general store along Main Street. If the district prospered, there would soon be a newspaper and a bank, a Knights of Pythias Lodge for the gentlemen, a Women's Christian Temperance Hall for the ladies, and for the children a baseball diamond beside the school. The towns were like islands. Beyond their last houses, the wide prairie rolled on for ever.

Dreams and Struggles

Canada's cities were developing as fast as the prairie farms. Soon there were factories and factory towns along the rail lines from Halifax to Vancouver. Cities seemed exciting places, with their street lights, electric streetcars, glamorous theatres, and amusement parks. Young people left family farms to find jobs in the factories, and not all immigrants headed to the Prairies. Thousands settled in the cities. Soon there were synagogues in Winnipeg, Sikh temples in Vancouver, Greek and Italian newspapers in Toronto, and Lebanese grocery stores in Halifax.

This 1897 view of Winnipeg shows Main Street south of City Hall.

Cities were not as wonderful as young farmers and immigrants dreamed they would be. Big factories were putting local enterprises and craft workshops out of business. Brewers and blacksmiths in every town found their wares replaced by factory-made products that the trains brought from the cities. Shopkeepers found their customers ordering from the Simpson's or Eaton's catalogues instead. Big manufacturers could make goods more quickly and cheaply, partly because they used powerful new machines run on electricity, but also because their employees worked long shifts six days a week, for low wages.

For most of the nineteenth century, unions were small,

This ice castle was the star attraction of the Montreal Winter Carnival of 1887. Today Quebec City's Carnaval *is the unchallenged champion for elaborate ice castles, but Montreal and Quebec City competed for years.*

The Wishing Books

For rural Canadians around the turn of the century, department store catalogues were a glimpse of another world, a world of glamorous clothes, marvellous household furnishings, stoves, books, games, and toys, as well as more practical items. There was in them everything the heart could desire – if the purse could afford it.

The day a catalogue reached a rural mailbox

was a great day. At home it would be pored over and kept in a special place while family members debated what they would buy.

When the next season's catalogue arrived, children were sometimes allowed to cut the old one up for scrapbooks or paper dolls. What was left often went to the outhouse as toilet paper. From start to finish the catalogues served their customers well!

local organizations of workers trying to improve their lives. In 1872, workers in Ontario towns and in Montreal campaigned to reduce the working day to nine hours. The printers struck at George Brown's newspaper, *The Globe*, and 1500 workers marched through the streets of Hamilton. In 1883, unions formed the first truly national organization, the Trades and Labor Congress of Canada, and by 1910 more than 100000 Canadian workers belonged to unions. Factory owners fought against unions and their demands for better pay and better working conditions. There would be violence and lockouts and setbacks for workers, but the union movement continued to grow.

A Voice for Women

There were always some workers who gave up the struggle and turned to drink for comfort. Rye whisky was cheap, and for a few hours poor people could forget their woes in a bottle. But if a man spent his wages on liquor, there was no welfare system and no protection for his family. Women had few legal rights, and so a drunken husband meant dire hardship, as well as abuse, for his wife and children. For that reason, women, along with religious and political leaders who cared about working people, preached the value of temperance. At first they simply wanted people to be careful – "temperate" – about how they drank, but soon temperance societies began to demand total bans on alcohol.

There were temperance societies throughout the country, and politicians won office on the temperance platform. Women could neither vote nor hold public office, but they became leaders in the movement for temperance. In Winnipeg, a teacher and writer named Nellie McClung fought for temperance – and began a lifelong battle for the rights of women. Women should have the same opportunities as men to make decisions about their lives and their children's lives, she argued. She insisted that women must

Nellie McClung

Nellie Mooney McClung was a writer and a champion of human rights. She was born in Ontario in 1873 and moved with her family to the Souris Valley in Manitoba when she was seven. She didn't begin school until she was ten.

At sixteen, Nellie McClung became a teacher. She wrote sixteen books, including her autobiography, *Clearing the West*, and many magazine articles. She began her political life fighting for temperance, and fought for the right of women to vote and own property. She also fought for laws to bring safety practices into factories.

Nellie McClung is remembered for her books and her devotion to human rights, but in her own time she was just as famous for her quick wit and sense of humour. Once when she was giving a speech during a Manitoba election campaign, a heckler yelled from the audience, "The prime minister would quit politics if a woman were ever elected."

"That proves what a purifying effect women would have on politics," retorted Nellie.

have the vote. It was no good pretending their fathers and husbands could be trusted to represent them.

In rural Ontario, Adelaide Hoodless began working for better education for women after her baby son died from drinking impure milk. In 1897 she founded the Women's Institute, in Stoney Creek, Ontario, as a place where women could share their knowledge of household management, health, and family nutrition. Women's Institutes were an instant success, and spread across the country and around the world. Mrs. Hoodless went on to help found the National Council of Women of Canada and the Victorian Order of Nurses. At first her organizations focussed on the traditional "women's sphere." Gradually their successes encouraged more women to campaign for votes and other rights that had been restricted to men.

Christian churches were the backbone of turn-of-the-century Canadian society. Most Canadians were Christians and churchgoers, and the churches were at the centre of most people's lives. Women got together in the Christian Temperance Union or the Dorcas Society, where they made

When Lucy Maud Montgomery wrote Anne of Green Gables *she probably didn't realize it would become the most popular Canadian book ever. First published in 1908, the famous story of red-haired Anne was enjoyed by so many people that Montgomery wrote sequel after sequel to please them.*

Emily Howard Stowe was the first woman to practise medicine in Canada.

clothes for missionary work. In the countryside, families often went to church with a packed lunch in the wagon. They shared a picnic, played games and heard a temperance speech with their neighbours after the morning service, and stayed for evening services before returning home. The family and the church were still the centres of life.

A Turn-of-the-Century Time Trip

Travel back in time and see what life was like for Canadian children around 1900. First imagine a boy, ten or twelve years old, who lives in a great stone house on Jarvis Street in Toronto. The house has a wide, curved drive in front, a coach house and stables in back. It has polished mahogany furniture, huge gilt-framed paintings on the walls, and thick Turkish carpets on the floors. Gas heat is piped into all the rooms through ornate vents with marble overmantels, and the rooms are bright with electric light. Hot and cold water runs from the taps in the kitchen and several bathrooms and there are indoor flush toilets.

Artist and photographer William Notman created this tobogganing scene in his studio. The scenery and the snow are all special effects, and the young models have been carefully posed. Notman created hundreds of scenes like this and hired talented artists to work on them.

Home Children

They were called "home children" but they were far from home. They came from orphanages in Britain, unwanted children or children whose parents couldn't feed them any more. Some of the people in charge of those orphanages thought the children would be better off where they could have fresh air and farm food, and so they advertised in Canada and Australia for people who would take a child.

There were willing people. Some took children out of the kindness of their hearts. But too many wanted them only as workers.

One man remembered his life many years later. "I was beat up with pieces of harness, pitchforks, anything that came in handy to hit me with, I got it. I didn't get enough to eat. . . . I used to swipe flour and sugar. . . . I never had a coat if it was raining. Just a grain sack over my shoulders and no shoes. I was supposed to go to school six months of the year, and in the seven years I only got to grade three. . . . They would buy me shoes that wouldn't fit. I used to cry with the pain."

Some of the children were actually starved. Some died. All in all the idea turned out to be a poor one. But between the 1860s and the 1930s, thousands of children were brought to Canada that way.

The boy goes to a private school where he learns English literature, composition, and spelling, British history, geography, mathematics, penmanship, Latin, and ancient Greek. His sisters' lessons are nearly the same, but their school teaches embroidery and piano playing instead of Greek. After school, the boys play cricket and lacrosse against teams from other boys' schools, while the girls practise archery and field hockey. In the evenings there are several hours of homework.

Saturdays bring him freedom. Perhaps the boy rides the trolley across town to meet a "chum." His sisters, however, are not allowed to travel on their own, and their Saturdays are often taken up with hairdressers or seamstresses who come to the house. Sometimes they have social calls to make with their mother.

The father of the family goes to his office every day but Sunday, and the mother manages the household. She sees that the cook, the housekeeper, the maids, and the houseboy all do their work properly. She organizes the family's social life, keeping track of invitations to dinner, mission society meetings at the church, and plays at the Royal Opera House that would be suitable for her children.

The thirteen-year-old maid who lives in the attic is not nearly so well off. She is up before dawn seven days a week (with just one day off a month) to help the cook with breakfast. Her bed is hard, the gas heat does not reach the third floor, and the small allowance of coal for her stove never really warms her room.

At least she has enough to eat, and she is glad to have her job, for her family could not afford to let her stay in school. Her father has a steady job in the brickyard. Her young brother makes a few cents a week selling *The Globe* on the street, and her older brother, a soldier in South Africa, sends home his pay. With the money their mother earns taking in washing and mending, the family manages to pay the rent and buy the coal for the two-room house on Sumach Street.

Some people are not so lucky. When their earnings do not pay the rent, they are turned out of their homes. The children live on the street, begging or stealing, and they may die of cold or malnutrition. Children are no longer hanged for stealing twenty-five cents (as one was in Saint John, New Brunswick, in 1824), but they can be whipped or jailed for minor offences. The first Children's Aid societies have just been started.

By this time Jewish immigrants from Poland, Russia, and Romania have settled in many parts of Canada. In Montreal or Winnipeg, the new arrivals have formed tightly knit groups, partly because Jewish law requires them to live close to their synagogue. Many live in walk-up apartments, often two families together. Mothers and aunts work on sewing machines, making clothes for the department

The Poor Children's Clinic at Toronto's Hospital for Sick Children in 1916. The sign is written in English and Yiddish, for Toronto's Jewish community was clustered around nearby Kensington Market.

Choosing sides for a hockey game in Sarnia, Ontario, in 1908.

stores. Fathers and uncles work in grocery or tailor shops or push peddler's carts around the city. The community is crowded and noisy, but it is hard to be lonely.

It is a very different life in a French-Canadian farmhouse a hundred kilometres east of Montreal. As in other rural areas, where many hands are needed about the farm, families are large, even though some of the children – and some of the mothers – are likely to die in childbirth. The children are up at four in the morning to milk the cows, feed the animals, and shovel out the barn. In summer, the older girls preserve vegetables, and the boys work in the long narrow fields with the men and horses.

Winter is easier. In the parish school, the nuns teach catechism, reading and writing in French, and a lot of the history of French Canada. The brightest children in the school go on to colleges, and many will become priests or nuns. A few of the boys have a piece of family-owned farmland waiting for them. Others will head to Montreal or the factory towns in New England, or off to lumber camps in the north woods.

The best times are midwinter Saturdays when the neighbours gather in the parlour. They sing and dance to the fiddle and hear the storytellers. Late in the evening

Many boys needed to work in the coal mines of Cape Breton to help support their families, and the mine owners liked the way they could fit into cramped tunnels deep underground.

they share sandwiches and sugar pie before everyone scrambles into the cutters for the ride home, still singing.

In a Cape Breton Island coal-mining town, a boy works underground, crouching in a mine shaft that runs out under the bottom of the ocean. Since the working day starts before dawn and ends after dusk, he sees the sun only on Sundays or during the few short weeks of summer. His lunch, a bit of bread and cheese called a "piece," always tastes of coal dust. Coal dust has gotten into his skin so deeply that it seems he cannot get it out, no matter how hard he scrubs in the big tin tub in front of the fireplace.

Many Canadian children, neither rich nor poor, were able to complete their schooling, though few went on to university. They lived in homes that were warm and comfortable, though they might not have electricity and the toilet was an outhouse at the back of the garden. Growing up in Canada around 1900 was so different for rich and poor, for settled families and immigrants, for city children and country children, that it was almost like living in different countries.

Into the North

There were no factories, schools, or churches in the Far North. Inuit had lived there, almost undisturbed, for a thousand years. Without consulting them, Canada had claimed all the land up to the North Pole in 1880, although no one knew what land was there. Between 1903 and 1906, Norwegian explorer Roald Amundsen manoeuvred his small ship, *Gjoa,* through the twisting, icy channels from the Arctic to the Pacific – through the long-sought Northwest Passage. During his voyage, Amundsen met many American, British, and Norwegian whalers pushing in from both east and west. They brought trade goods to the Inuit, but they also brought disease. In 1900 one whaling ship carried sickness to the Sadlermiut Inuit of Hudson Bay – and they all died.

Far to the south, in Ottawa, Wilfrid Laurier's government began to think that Canada had to take charge of the North. If it did not, the Americans surely would. On July 1, 1909, Captain Joseph Bernier planted Canada's flag at Winter Harbour on Melville Island in the heart of the Arctic Islands. His ship, the *Arctic,* was still frozen in the ice, but Bernier was a master sailor and an Arctic veteran, and he was confident. Boldly he laid claim to every inch of the Arctic for Canada.

A swimming class in the Don River at Toronto, 1909.

In 1913, Vilhjalmur Stefansson led another Canadian expedition to the Arctic. Stef, as he liked to be called, had been born in Manitoba's Icelandic settlement and raised in the United States. He loved the North. He called it "the friendly Arctic," and said it was a wonderful place for those willing to adapt to it as he did.

Stef had lived among the Inuit, learning their language and how they were able to live in harmony with the North. He travelled by dogsled instead of taking large ships into the ice. He hunted as he went, trusting the land and sea instead of hauling huge stocks of food. Ranging across the North, he added a whole group of islands to the map of Canada. When he found his first uncharted island in June 1915, Stef and his men put aside their usual raw sealmeat and shared the only treat they had – some biscuit crumbs and malted milk. Before he headed south in 1918, Stefansson filled in the last large blank on the map of Canada.

Billy Stark bought a Curtiss biplane in 1912 and brought it home to Vancouver, where crowds gathered to watch him fly. A herd of cattle complicated his landing at Hastings Park on May 4. Fortunately, Stark (and the cows) survived, and his airplane was soon repaired.

Hundreds of Torontonians flooded the streets on Pretoria Day, June 5, 1901, to celebrate the end of the South African War.

The Canadians and the Empire

As Canada grew, differences among Canadians seemed to become greater, not less. Those who dreamed of building a new nationality from ocean to ocean regretted these differences, and Canada's diversity made life hard for its political leaders. "This is a difficult country to govern," Wilfrid Laurier said ruefully.

In Laurier's time, many Canadians of British descent looked as much to London as to Ottawa for leadership. They called themselves "imperialists." Britain governed the most powerful empire in the world. Canadian imperialists did not want to be independent, but to share in running the whole empire. In 1899, when Britain went to war against the Dutch-speaking Boer settlers of South Africa, the imperialists wanted Canadians to fight alongside the British. Later they argued that Canada should buy ships for the British navy instead of building a Canadian navy.

A young Montreal newspaperman named Henri Bourassa fought the ideas of the imperialists. He hoped that French Canadians and English Canadians would build an independent Canada together. Quebeckers cheered when he asked if the English Canadians intended to be colonials forever. In the Boer War, he sympathized with the Boers more than with the British.

Wilfrid Laurier had to steer a careful course, for he needed the support of both English Canada and Quebec. During the Boer War, his government supported Canadian volunteers who went to South Africa, and many did. But he also began building a Canadian navy – which the imperialists sneered at as "the tin-pot navy."

Britain eventually won the South African war, but the tough resistance of the Boer forces embarrassed the mighty British army. Queen Victoria, the symbol of imperial might and glory for over sixty years, died in 1901. As the world moved into the twentieth century, Canada's interests

Silver Dart, *piloted by J.A.D. McCurdy, took off from the frozen surface of Baddeck Bay, Nova Scotia, on February 23, 1909. It was the first aircraft flight in Canada. Within a few years, planes were buzzing through the skies all over Canada.*

Stephen Leacock

"Lord Ronald said nothing; he flung himself from the room, flung himself upon his horse and rode madly off in all directions." Stephen Leacock wrote that in 1911, and people all over the world laughed. Leacock was a professor at McGill University who wrote serious books about economics, but he became much more famous for his funny books. When people said being funny must be easy, he half-agreed. "You just jot down ideas as they occur to you," he said. "The jotting is simplicity itself – it is the occurring which is difficult."

Some of Leacock's best stories are set in the imaginary town of Mariposa. He based Mariposa on Orillia, Ontario, where his summer home still stands.

moved more and more towards the United States.

Canada's relations with the United States were almost as complicated as those with Britain and its empire. Laurier had continued Macdonald's National Policy of tariffs to protect Canadian factories. Then, in 1911, he proposed to switch paths completely – free trade with the Americans became the new policy.

"Follow my white plume," cried Laurier, whose hair had gone white while he was prime minister. But few did. Bourassa had challenged his popularity in Quebec, and imperialists rejected him in English Canada. An American politician made matters worse for Laurier by predicting that free trade would be only the first step. Soon, he boasted, "the American flag will float over every square foot of the British North American possessions clear to the North Pole."

In the Canada of 1911, that was enough to kill the notion of free trade with the Americans. Laurier's luck had run out. Canadians threw out the Liberal Party, and Laurier was back to being leader of the Opposition. His sunny days were ending, and stormy times were coming to Canada.

Chronology

About 75 million years ago Dinosaurs live in steamy forests and warm seas that cover much of what we now call Canada.

About 20 000 years ago The first human inhabitants of North America probably cross from Siberia by land bridge as the last Ice Age draws to a close.

About 1000 years ago Native people of southern Ontario begin to plant and harvest corn. The Thule people – ancestors of the Inuit – migrate east across Arctic Canada.

About 1000 years ago Leif Ericsson's first voyage to Vinland. A Norse colony is established in Vinland, but lasts only a couple of years.

About 600 years ago Five Iroquois nations form the powerful Confederacy of the Longhouse.

1497, 1498 John Cabot (Giovanni Caboto) of Genoa makes two voyages for England to the fishing grounds off Newfoundland.

1534 Jacques Cartier explores the coasts of Newfoundland, Prince Edward Island, and New Brunswick. He lands on the Gaspé Peninsula and claims the land for France.

1535 Cartier journeys up the St. Lawrence to the Native settlements of Stadacona and Hochelaga. He gives Canada its name (from the Indian word *kanata*, meaning "village").

1576 Martin Frobisher journeys as far as Frobisher Bay, Baffin Island, in his search for the Northwest Passage.

1583 Sir Humphrey Gilbert visits Newfoundland and claims it for England.

1604 Pierre Du Gua de Monts and Samuel de Champlain establish a colony in Nova Scotia. Marc Lescarbot starts the first library and first French school for Native people. In 1606 he produces the first play in Canada.

1608 Samuel de Champlain founds a permanent French colony at Quebec.

1610–1611 Explorer Henry Hudson is set adrift by his mutinous crew in Hudson Bay.

1615 The first Roman Catholic missionaries try to convert the Native people to Christianity.

1616 Champlain completes eight years of exploration, travelling as far west as Georgian Bay. The French and Hurons form an alliance.

1617 Louis and Marie Hébert and their children become the first French settlers to farm land in New France.

1630s The first French schools are founded in Quebec by religious orders.

1642 Ville-Marie (Montreal) is founded by Paul de Maisonneuve.

1645 The Hôtel-Dieu Hospital in Ville-Marie, founded by Jeanne Mance, is completed.

1649 War between the Huron and Iroquois confederacies leads to the destruction of the Huron nation. The Iroquois begin raids on New France.

1663 King Louis XIV decides to rebuild New France. He sends a governor and troops to protect the colony, an intendant (Jean Talon) to administer it, and settlers to increase its population.

1670 The English king grants a charter to the Hudson's Bay Company, giving it exclusive trading rights to vast territory drained by rivers that flow into Hudson Bay.

1682 René-Robert Cavelier de La Salle reaches the mouth of the Mississippi, and claims for France all the land through which the river and its tributaries flow.

Early 1700s Horses come to the northern plains, and the Native peoples begin to ride on horseback.

1713 A peace treaty forces France to turn over Newfoundland and Acadia to Britain. The French begin construction of Louisbourg, strongest fortress in North America, on Cape Breton Island.

1726 The first English school in Newfoundland is established, known as "the school for poor people."

1743 Louis-Joseph, explores westward in search of the "Western Sea," crossing the plains almost to the Rocky Mountains.

1749 The British found Halifax as a naval and military post; about 3000 people settle there in one year.

March 25, 1752 First issue of the *Halifax Gazette*, Canada's first newspaper.

1755 The expulsion of the Acadians by the British begins: 6000–10 000 Acadians driven from their homes.

1756–1763 The Seven Years' War between Great Britain and France, fought partly in their North American colonies: ***July 8, 1758*** French troops, under the command of Louis-Joseph de Montcalm, win victory over the British at Carillon (Ticonderoga). ***July 26, 1758*** The British capture Louisbourg from the French. ***September 13, 1759*** At the Battle of the Plains of Abraham, Quebec falls to the British. Both commanders, Wolfe and Montcalm, are killed. ***September 8, 1760*** New France surrenders to the British. ***1763*** New France becomes a British colony called Quebec.

1763 Alliance of Native nations under Pontiac, chief of the Ottawa, makes war on the British, seizing many forts and trading posts.

1769 Prince Edward Island, formerly part of Nova Scotia, becomes separate British colony.

1770–1772 Samuel Hearne, guided by Chipewyan leader Matonabbee, explores the Coppermine and Slave rivers and Great Slave Lake. He is the first white man to reach the Arctic Ocean overland.

1773 Scottish settlers reach Pictou, Nova Scotia, aboard the *Hector*.

1774 Quebec Act is passed by British

Parliament, recognizing the French Canadians' right to preserve their language, religion, and civil law.

1775–1783 The American Revolution gains independence from Great Britain for the Thirteen Colonies. The people of Quebec, Nova Scotia, and Prince Edward Island decide against joining the revolution.

December 31, 1775 American invaders under General Montgomery assault Quebec. The city is under siege until spring, when British reinforcements arrive.

1776 The fur traders of Montreal band together in the North West Company to compete with the traders of the Hudson's Bay Company.

1778 Captain James Cook explores the Pacific Coast from Nootka (Yuquot Cove) to the Bering Strait.

1783 Immigration of 40 000 United Empire Loyalists from the Thirteen Colonies. Most settle in Nova Scotia, Quebec, and New Brunswick (established as a colony separate from Nova Scotia in 1784). Three thousand Black Loyalists settle near Shelburne, Nova Scotia.

1784 After helping the British during the American Revolution, the Iroquois are given two land grants. Thayendanegea (Joseph Brant) settles his followers at the Six Nations Reserve, near Brantford.

1791 Quebec is divided into two colonies, Upper and Lower Canada, each with its own Assembly.

1792, 1793, 1794 Captain George Vancouver makes summer voyages to explore the coasts of mainland British Columbia and Vancouver Island.

1793 By canoe and on foot, Alexander Mackenzie crosses the Rocky Mountains and the Coast Range, reaching the Pacific Ocean on July 22.

1793 York (now Toronto) founded by John Graves Simcoe, lieutenant-governor of Upper Canada.

1803 First paper mill established in Lower Canada, producing paper from cloth rags.

1808 Simon Fraser travels the Fraser River for 1360 km to reach the Pacific Ocean on July 2.

1811 Lord Selkirk plans a settlement of Highland Scots in Red River area, near present site of Winnipeg. First settlers arrive at Hudson Bay in the fall of 1811.

1812–1814 The War of 1812, between the United States and Britain: ***August 16, 1812*** Detroit surrenders to British general Isaac Brock and Tecumseh, leader of the Native nations allied to Britain. ***October 13, 1812*** Brock is killed during the Battle of Queenston Heights. ***June 22, 1813*** Laura Secord overhears American troops planning an attack, and walks 30 km, crossing enemy lines, to warn Colonel James FitzGibbon. Two days later, the Americans are ambushed and surrender to FitzGibbon. ***October 5, 1813*** Tecumseh dies during the British defeat at Moraviantown. ***December 24, 1814*** The Treaty of Ghent officially ends the war.

June 6, 1829 Shawnandithit, the last of the Beothuks, dies at about age twenty-eight in St. John's, Newfoundland.

1830 Escaped slaves Josiah and Charlotte Henson and their children journey north from Maryland to Canada. The Hensons later help found a community of ex-slaves called Dawn, near Dresden, Ontario.

1832 The Rideau Canal, built by Colonel John By, opens; the community of Bytown (later Ottawa) grows out of the camp for the canal workers.

1836 The first railway in Canada opens, running from La Prairie to St. John's, Quebec.

1837 Rebellions in Upper and Lower Canada are put down by government troops. Rebel leaders, Louis-Joseph Papineau of Lower Canada and William Lyon Mackenzie of Upper Canada, are forced to flee.

1838 Lord Durham comes to Canada as governor. He recommends that the governments of the colonies should be chosen by the people's elected representatives.

1840 *Britannia* – the first ship of the Cunard Line, founded by Samuel Cunard of Halifax – arrives in Halifax harbour with transatlantic mail.

1841 The Act of Union unites Upper and Lower Canada (which became Canada West and Canada East) into the Province of Canada, under one government, with Kingston as capital.

1842 Charles Fenerty of Sackville, New Brunswick, discovers a practical way to make paper from wood pulp. Today the pulp and paper industry is Canada's largest manufacturing industry, and Canada exports more pulp and paper than any other country in the world.

1843 James Douglas of the Hudson's Bay Company founds Victoria on Vancouver Island.

1845 Sir John Franklin and his crew disappear in the Arctic while seeking the Northwest Passage.

1846 Geologist and chemist Abraham Gesner of Nova Scotia invents kerosene oil and becomes the founder of the modern petroleum industry.

1851 Canada's first postage stamp is issued, a three-penny stamp with a beaver on it.

1856 Timothy Eaton opens his first general store, in Kirkton, Ontario. He later opens a store at the corner of Queen and Yonge in Toronto.

1857 Queen Victoria chooses Ottawa as the new capital of the United Province of Canada.

1858 Gold is discovered in the sandbars of the Fraser River. Some twenty thousand miners rush to the area, and it comes under British rule as the colony of British Columbia.

1859 The French acrobat Blondin crosses Niagara Falls on a tightrope. On later walks, he crosses the falls on stilts, blindfolded, and with his feet in a sack.

1864 Confederation conferences in Charlottetown, Prince Edward Island, September 1–9, and in Quebec, October 10–29. Delegates hammer out the conditions for union of British North American colonies.

March 29, 1867 The British North America Act is passed by Britain's Parliament, providing for Canada's Confederation.

July 1, 1867 Confederation: New Brunswick, Nova Scotia, Quebec, and Ontario form the Dominion of Canada, and John A. Macdonald becomes the first prime minister.

1867 Emily Stowe, the first woman doctor in Canada, begins to practise medicine in Toronto.

1869 The Métis of Red River rebel, under Louis Riel, after their region is purchased by Canada from the Hudson's Bay Company.

July 15, 1870 Manitoba joins Confederation, much smaller than today's Manitoba.

1870 As buffalo become scarce, the last tribal war is fought on the Prairies between the Cree and the Blackfoot over hunting territories.

July 20, 1871 British Columbia joins Confederation.

May 1873 American whisky traders kill fifty-six Assiniboine in the Cypress Hills of the southern Prairies. The North-West Mounted Police (later the RCMP) is formed to keep order in the new Canadian territories.

1873 Prime Minister Sir John A. Macdonald resigns as a result of scandal over the partial financing of the Conservative election campaign by the Canadian Pacific Railway Company.

July 1, 1873 Prince Edward Island joins Confederation.

August 1876 Scottish-born Alexander Graham Bell, who has been working on the invention of the telephone since 1874, makes the world's first long-distance call, from Brantford to Paris, Ontario.

1879 The first organized games of hockey, using a flat puck, are played by McGill University students in Montreal. Before this, hockey-like games have been played on ice with a ball.

1880 Britain transfers the Arctic, which it claims to own, to Canada, completing Canada's modern boundaries – except for Newfoundland and Labrador.

1884 A system of international standard time and official time zones, advocated by Canadian engineer Sir Sandford Fleming, is adopted.

1885 The North-West Rebellion is led by Louis Riel and Gabriel Dumont. After early victories for the Métis rebels, the rebellion is crushed by troops who arrive on the newly built railway.

November 7, 1885 The last spike of the Canadian Pacific Railway main line is driven at Craigellachie, B.C. The next year, Vancouver is founded as the railway's western terminus.

1891 The City of Toronto establishes the first Children's Aid Society in Canada.

1893 Lord Stanley, the governor general, donates the Stanley Cup as a hockey trophy.

1896 Gold is discovered in the Klondike. By the next year, 100 000 people are rushing to the Yukon in the hope of getting rich.

1899–1902 The Boer War in South Africa is fought between Dutch Afrikaners (Boers) and the British. Seven thousand Canadian volunteers fight on the British side.

September 1, 1905 Saskatchewan and Alberta join Confederation. Immigrants rush to settle on the plains, mainly as wheat farmers.

1906 Norwegian Roald Amundsen, in the schooner *Gjoa*, finds his way through the Northwest Passage to the Pacific.

1907 Tom Longboat, an Onondaga from the Six Nations Reserve and a world champion distance runner, wins the Boston Marathon in record time. In 1906 he won a 12-mile (almost 20 km) race against a horse.

1908 *Anne of Green Gables*, by Lucy Maud Montgomery, is published. In the next ninety years the book sells more than a million copies, is made into a television movie, and becomes a popular musical.

1909 The first powered, heavier-than-air flight in Canada is made by J.A.D. McCurdy in the *Silver Dart*. The biplane flew almost a kilometre.

1909 The first Grey Cup game; the University of Toronto football team defeats Toronto Parkdale. A trophy has been donated by the governor general, Earl Grey.

1911 A proposal for free trade between the United States and Canada is rejected in a fiercely contested general election. The Liberal government, under Wilfrid Laurier, is replaced by a Conservative government led by Sir William Borden.

1913 Vilhjalmur Stefansson leads a Canadian expedition to the Arctic, and explores the North by deliberately drifting on ice floes.

1914–1918 The First World War. Britain declares war on Germany on behalf of the British Empire, including Canada. ***April 22–May 25, 1915*** Battle of Ypres (Belgium). The first major battle fought by Canadian troops. They stand their ground against poison-gas attacks. ***April 9–14, 1917*** Battle of Vimy Ridge (France). A Canadian victory, at cost of more than 10 000 killed or wounded. ***October 26–November 7, 1917*** Passchendaele (Belgium). A Canadian victory, at the cost of more than 15 000 casualties. Nine Victoria Crosses are awarded to

Canadians. ***1917*** Flying ace Billy Bishop of Owen Sound, Ontario, wins the Victoria Cross for attacking a German airfield single-handed.

November 26, 1917 The National Hockey League is established in Montreal. The original teams are: Montreal Canadiens, Montreal Wanderers, Ottawa Senators, and Toronto Arenas.

1917 Sir William Borden leads a unionist coalition, which combines support by Conservatives and western Liberals, into a wartime election against the Laurier Liberals. Borden wins.

December 6, 1917 A French munitions ship explodes in Halifax harbour, flattening the city, killing 1600, and injuring 9000.

1918 Women win the right to vote in federal elections.

May 15–June 25, 1919 The Winnipeg General Strike. A strike in the building and metal trades spreads to other unions, and 30 000 workers stop work, crippling the city.

August 1919 Following the death of Laurier, William Lyon Mackenzie King is chosen to be leader of the Liberal Party.

1920 The Group of Seven artists hold their first exhibition, in Toronto.

1921 Agnes Macphail of Owen Sound, Ontario, becomes the first woman elected to the House of Commons, in the first election since women gained the vote.

1923 The Nobel Prize for Medicine is awarded to doctors Frederick Banting and J.J.R. Macleod. Along with Dr. Charles Best and others, Banting discovered insulin as a treatment for diabetes.

1927 The first government old-age pension pays up to $20 per month.

July 1, 1927 To celebrate Canada's Diamond jubilee (sixtieth birthday), the first coast-to-coast radio broadcast is made.

1928 At the first Olympics in which women may compete, a Canadian women's six-member track team wins one bronze, two silver, and two gold medals.

1929 England's Privy Council rules that women are indeed "persons," and therefore can be appointed to the Canadian Senate. The next year, Cairine Wilson becomes Canada's first woman senator.

October 29, 1929 North American stock markets crash and the Great Depression begins.

1930 R.B. Bennett leads the Conservative Party to victory over William Lyon Mackenzie King's Liberals as the country is plunged into the Great Depression.

November 2, 1936 The Canadian Broadcasting Corporation is established.

April 1, 1939 Trans-Canada Airlines (later Air Canada) makes the first scheduled passenger flight from Vancouver to Montreal.

1939–1945 The Second World War. After Germany invades Poland, Britain and Canada declare war. ***December 7, 1941*** The Japanese attack U.S. naval base at Pearl Harbor, and Canada declares war on Japan. ***December 1941*** The Fall of Hong Kong. More than 500 Canadians die in battle or of ill-treatment in Japanese prison camps. ***1942*** Twenty-two thousand Japanese Canadians are rounded up by RCMP and placed in work camps. ***August 19, 1942*** In a disastrous raid on Dieppe, France, 900 out of 5000 Canadians are killed and almost 2000 are taken prisoner. ***May–October 1942*** German submarines in the Gulf of St. Lawrence sink twenty-three Allied ships, with a loss of 258 lives. The gulf is then closed to ocean shipping until 1944. ***July 1943*** Canadian troops invade Sicily and, with other Allied troops, fight their way north through Italy. They reach Rome on June 4, 1944. ***June 6, 1944 (D day)*** Canadian troops, along with British and Americans, land successfully on the coast of France and begin to drive the Germans back.

July 1941 The first national unemployment-insurance program comes into operation.

1945 Family-allowance payments begin. All families receive a monthly sum for each child under sixteen who is in school.

February 1947 Prospectors strike oil in Leduc, Alberta, beginning the Alberta oil boom.

March 31, 1949 Newfoundland and Labrador join Confederation as the tenth province.

1949 William Lyon Mackenzie King, Canada's longest-serving prime minister, retires at the age of 74.

1950–1954 The Korean War. Twenty-seven thousand Canadians serve and more than 1600 are killed or wounded.

1950 Inuit win the right to vote in federal elections.

1952 Vincent Massey becomes the first Canadian-born governor general since Pierre Rigaud de Vaudreuil governed New France.

September 6, 1952 The first Canadian scheduled TV broadcast.

September 9, 1954 Marilyn Bell, age sixteen, is the first person to swim Lake Ontario.

1957 Lester Pearson wins the Nobel Peace Prize for proposing a United Nations peacekeeping force to prevent war over control of the Suez Canal.

1957 John George Diefenbaker leads the Conservative Party to decisive victory over Louis St. Laurent's Liberals in a federal election, winning more seats in the House of Commons than any party has before.

October 23, 1958 The Springhill Mining Disaster. Shifting rock kills seventy-four coal miners. Some of the survivors are trapped for eight days before being rescued.

June 26, 1959 Queen Elizabeth II and U.S. President Dwight Eisenhower officially open the St. Lawrence Seaway, which lets ocean vessels reach the Great Lakes.

1960 Native people living on reserves get the right to vote in federal elections.

1960 Social changes and a new government in Quebec lead to the beginning of Quebec's "Quiet Revolution." Stirrings of interest in independence for Quebec soon follow.

1962 Saskatchewan is the first province to have medical insurance covering doctors' bills. In 1966, Parliament passes legislation to establish a national medicare program. By 1972, all provinces and territories have joined the program.

September 29, 1962 The first Canadian satellite, *Alouette I*, is launched by the American space agency.

1963 The FLQ, a terrorist group dedicated to revolution to establish an independent Quebec, explodes bombs in Montreal.

February 15, 1965 Canada gets a new red-and-white, maple leaf flag.

1967 Canada celebrates a hundred years of Confederation. Across the country, communities sponsor centennial projects. In Ottawa, on July 1, Queen Elizabeth II cuts a giant birthday cake.

April–October 1967 Expo 67, the Montreal world's fair, attracts more than 55 million visitors.

1968 René Lévesque founds the Parti Québécois, with the goal of making Quebec a "sovereign" (independent) state "associated" with Canada.

1968 Pierre Elliott Trudeau succeeds Lester Pearson as prime minister. "Trudeaumania" sweeps the country in the subsequent federal election.

1970 Voting age lowered from twenty-one to eighteen.

1970 The October Crisis. After the FLQ kidnaps a Quebec government minister and a British trade commissioner, Prime Minister Trudeau invokes the War Measures Act, which allows Canadians to be arrested and held without being charged.

1971 Gerhard Herzberg of Ottawa wins the Nobel Prize for Chemistry.

1976 René Lévesque and the Parti Québécois are elected in Quebec.

1976 Wayne Gretzky, age seventeen, plays hockey for the Edmonton Oilers; he is the youngest person in North America playing a major-league sport.

April 12, 1980 Terry Fox begins his cross-country run, the "Marathon of Hope." On September 1, he is forced to stop the run when his cancer returns.

May 15, 1980 Quebec voters reject "sovereignty-association" in favour of renewed Confederation.

November 1981 First flight of the Canadian Remote Manipulator System (Canadarm) on the space shuttle. The highly computerized 15m arm can be operated from inside the shuttle to release, rescue, and repair satellites.

November 5, 1981 The federal government and every province except Quebec reach agreement for patriating the Canadian constitution (bringing it to Canada from Great Britain).

April 17, 1982 Canada gets a new Constitution Act, including a Charter of Rights and Freedoms.

May 14, 1984 Jeanne Sauvé is Canada's first woman governor general.

1984 At the Summer Olympics in Los Angeles, Canada wins its greatest-ever number of gold medals: ten, including two for swimmer Alex Baumann.

October 5, 1984 Astronaut Marc Garneau, aboard the U.S. space shuttle *Challenger*, becomes the first Canadian in space.

March 21, 1985 Wheelchair athlete Rick Hansen leaves Vancouver on a round-the-world "Man in Motion" tour to raise money for spinal-cord research and wheelchair sports.

1986 John Polanyi of Toronto is co-winner of the Nobel Prize for Chemistry.

May–October 1986 Expo 86, the Vancouver world's fair, attracts more than 20 million visitors.

April 30, 1987 Ten provincial premiers and Prime Minister Brian Mulroney agree to the Meech Lake Accord, which would make large changes to Canada's Constitution and address Quebec's concerns. It dies in June 1991, when both Newfoundland and Manitoba refuse to endorse it.

February 13–28, 1988 The Calgary Winter Olympics. Canada wins two silver medals (Brian Orser and Elizabeth Manley, for figure skating) and three bronze medals.

January 1, 1989 After a federal election fought over the issue of free trade, the free-trade agreement between Canada and the United States comes into effect, gradually ending controls on trade and investment between the two countries.

December 2, 1989 Audrey McLaughlin becomes the first woman leader of a federal party – the New Democratic Party.

April 1990 The federal government settles a land claim with the Inuit that will give them 350 000 square km of territory in the North, to be called Nunavut.

Summer 1990 A land dispute causes a 78-day armed confrontation between Mohawks and the army on a reserve near Oka, Quebec.

January–February 1991 War in the Persian Gulf. Canada sends three warships, twenty-six fighter jets, and 2400 people to the Persian Gulf as part of a United Nations effort to force Iraqi troops to withdraw from Kuwait.

January 22, 1992 Dr. Roberta Bondar becomes the first Canadian woman in space, aboard the U.S. space shuttle *Discovery*.

August 28, 1992 Canadian leaders adopt the Charlottetown Accord to reform Canada's constitution, but in a national referendum in October, Canadians reject it.

October 24, 1992 Toronto's Blue Jays became the first Canadian team to win baseball's World Series.

1993 Canada, with Kurt Browning (gold), Elvis Stojko (silver), and Isabelle Brasseur and Lloyd Eisler (gold), has its best skating World Championship since 1962.

June 25, 1993 Kim Campbell, the new Conservative party leader, becomes Canada's first female prime minister, but in October, Jean Chrétien's Liberals win the general election.

1994 The North American Free Trade Agreement (NAFTA) comes into effect, linking Canada, the United States, and Mexico in a new economic partnership.

September 15, 1994 Separatist Jacques Parizeau becomes the premier of Quebec.

1995 "Turbot war" erupts when Canada arrests a Spanish ship in a bid to prevent European fleets from over-harvesting Newfoundland fish stocks.

1995 Donovan Bailey becomes "the world's fastest man" when he breaks the record for the 100-metre race.

October 30, 1995 Quebec votes in a referendum on sovereignty and the federalists win a razor-thin victory.

January 29, 1996 Lucien Bouchard is sworn in as the new premier of Quebec.

May 19, 1996 Astronaut Marc Garneau makes his second trip into space.

1996 Lucien Bouchard becomes leader of the separatist Parti Québécois and premier of Quebec.

Astronaut Marc Garneau makes his second trip into space.

Donovan Bailey wins the 100-metre gold medal at the Atlanta Olympics.

1997 Jean Chrétien's Liberal Party wins re-election in the federal election.

The "flood of the century" hits Manitoba's Red River valley, but "the big ditch" built many years earlier protects Winnipeg.

1998 An extraordinary ice storm devastates the Montreal region and eastern Ontario, destroying trees and leaving millions in cold and darkness as electrical systems collapse.

1999 Eaton's, a familiar name to Canadian shoppers for more than 100 years, goes out of business.

The new territory of Nunavut is established in Canada's eastern Arctic.

Adrienne Clarkson becomes Governor General of Canada.

2000 Canada enters a new millennium.

2001 Security alerts across Canada after terrorist attacks of September 11 on New York City and Washington.

2002 Canadian forces take up combat mission in Afghanistan.

Canada signs the Kyoto Accord, a global effort to reduce the greenhouse gases that cause global warming.

2003 Jean Chrétien retires as prime minister and is succeeded by Paul Martin.

SARS epidemic kills more than thirty people and causes fear in Toronto and Vancouver.

Hurricane Juan damages Halifax.

2004 The "Sponsorship Scandal" damages the reputation of the Liberal government.

CBC Television's "Greatest Canadian" contest chooses Tommy Douglas.

Same-sex marriages become legal throughout Canada.

2005 Canada sends aid to Asian countries devastated by New Year's Eve tsunami.

Michaëlle Jean becomes Governor General.

Canadian Steve Nash named National Basketball Association's Most Valuable Player.

2006 The Conservative party forms a minority government and Stephen Harper becomes prime minister of Canada.

"King Ralph" Klein retires after 14 years as premier of Alberta.

2007 Census results show Canada had 31 612 897 people in 2006.

Publishers' Acknowledgments

The publishers wish to acknowledge the financial support of the Canadian Studies and Special Projects Directorate of the Department of the Secretary of State of Canada.

Basil Johnston, O. Ont., of the Department of Ethnology of the Royal Ontario Museum read and commented upon an early draft of the manuscript. On numerous occasions, Jack Granatstein generously provided advice.

For kind permission to reprint material used herein, the publishers are grateful to: Farley Mowat, for the excerpt from Never Cry Wolf; and Ariel Rogers for the excerpt from the Stan Rogers song "Northwest Passage."

The excerpt from David Thompson's Narrative is taken from John Warkentin, ed., *The Western Interior of Canada: A Record of Geographical Discovery*, 1612–1917, Carleton Library No. 15 (Toronto and Montreal: McClelland and Stewart Limited, 1964, 1969), pp. 102-103. The passage from *Roughing It in the Bush*, by Susanna Moodie, is from the New Canadian Library edition, No. 31 (Toronto: McClelland and Stewart Limited, 1962, 1970), p. 194.

Authors' and Illustrator's Acknowledgments

Malcolm Lester and Louise Dennys first suggested this book to us, and we began it with the support of the editorial team they assembled at Lester & Orpen Dennys, particularly Carol Martin and Sandra LaFortune. We completed it with the help of Kathy Lowinger at Lester Publishing and Phyllis Bruce and her staff at Key Porter Books, who handled a thousand last-minute details and guided the manuscript through to publication.

The authors wish to thank the Ontario Arts Council for a grant that helped them to complete the work. We also thank the staffs of the public libraries of Trenton and Kitchener, Ontario, and of the Metropolitan Toronto Central Reference Library, as well as many writers, readers, and friends who listened well.

The illustrator would like to thank the staff of the Kitchener Public Library, especially those in the Grace Schmidt Room. Staff at many other institutions were enormously helpful: at the Canadian Museum of Civilization, Dr. Bryan C. Gordon, Dr. David Keenlyside, and their fellow curators; at Parks Canada, Richard Lindo and René Chartrand; at Fort Edmonton Park, Jane Repp; at the National Aviation Museum, Rénald Fortier. I received assistance from the archives of the CPR; Fort Ticonderoga, N.Y.; Ste-Marie Among the Hurons; Historic Naval and Military Establishments at Penetanguishene; the Citadel, Halifax; the Royal Ontario Museum (Sigmund Samuel Collection); and from most of the provincial archives.

I would also like to express my appreciation to Commander Tony German, RCN (Ret.), and to the late J. Merle Smith, my father-in-law, who inspired me with his love for historical illustrations.

Picture Credits

All the illustrations are by Alan Daniel, with the exception of those credited below. The following abbreviations have been used:

AO: Archives of Ontario, Toronto
BCARS: British Columbia Archives & Records Service
BCARS/V: British Columbia Archives and Records Service/Visual Records Unit
CL: The Confederation Life Gallery of Canadian History
CPR: Canadian Pacific Railway Corporate Archives
CTA: City of Toronto Archives/James Collection
GA: Glenbow Archives, Calgary
MM: McCord Museum of Canadian History, McGill University, Montreal
MTL: Metropolitan Toronto Reference Library, Toronto
MTL/JRR: ———/John Ross Robertson Collection
NAC: National Archives of Canada
NPA/MM: Notman Photographic Archives/McCord Museum of Canadian History
ROM: Royal Ontario Museum, Toronto
ROM/C: ———/Canadiana Department
ROM/E: ———/Ethnology Department

Chapter One

Page 3: A.J. Miller/NAC/C-403; 5: Dorothy Siemens; 6: William Armstrong/NAC/C-19041; 9: GA; 11: Henry James Warre/NAC/C-1629; 12: William Hind/NAC/C-13965; 13: C.W. Jefferys/NAC/C-16750; 14: Manitoba Archives, John Kerr Collection; 15: NPA/MM/78494-BI; 116:NGC/#6920/ Transferred from the Parliament of Canada, 1955; 17: Royal Geographic Society, London/T129; 20: MM/M605; 21, top: GA/985.221.168; bottom: GA/M1083; 22: Samuel G. Cresswell/MTL; 23: Owen Beattie/University of Alberta/CP.

Chapter Two

Page 29: Fraser Clark; 30: ROM/E/912.1.93; 31: George Mercer Dawson/NAC/PA-37756; 32: Fraser Clark; 145: Royal British Columbia Museum/#1908; 34: BCARS/V/PDP2252; 35, bottom: BCARS/V/HP6462; 39: BCARS/V/PDP2258; 40: BCARS/V/HP127; 42: BCARS/HP2654; 43: MTL/JRR/MTL2313; 44: BCARS/HP759; 45: BCARS/HP7106; 46: BCARS/HP92108; 47: BCARS/HP17933.

Chapter Three

Page 163: C. Williams/NAC/C-5086; 52: Cincinnati Art Museum, Subscription Fund Purchase, #1927.26; 53: Hunter & Co., Toronto/NAC/C-9553; 54, top: MTL/T13731; bottom: NAC/PA-11566; 55: MTL/JRR; 56-57: ISTC; 59: G.H. Andrews, Niagara Falls with Terrapin Tower/ROM/C/962.111.3; 60: CL; 61: William Notman & Son, Montreal/NAC/C-6166; 62: NAC/C-22002; 63: Thomas Kitchin/FL; 65: NAC/C-15369; 66: Manitoba Museum of Man & Nature/#3661; 67: GA/NA1406-71; 68: NAC/PA-66544; 69: Thomas Kitchin/FL; 70: GA/NA1104-1; 72: PAA/#A12006; 74: J.W. Bengough/NAC/C-8449; 75: BCARS/HP72553; 78-79: Alan Daniel/Courtesy of The Reader's Digest Association (Canada) Ltd.; 79: CPR/#1960; 80, top: Sergt. Grundy/NAC/C-2424; bottom: Robert William Rutherford/NAC/C-2769; 81, top: GA/NA-428-1; bottom: CPR.

Chapter Four

Page 84: NAC/C-932; 85: NAC/PA-68351; 86, top: Dartmouth Heritage Museum; bottom: Special Collections Division, University of Washington Libraries, photo by Cantwell, #46; 87: CL; 88: NAC/C-23354; 89: NAC/C-9671; 90: GA; 91: AGO/Gift from the Fund of the T. Eaton Co. Ltd. for Canadian Works of Art, 1948; 92: GA/NA-978-4; 93: NAC/C-6605; 94: Thomas Kitchin/FL; 95, top: Provincial Archives of Manitoba/N10911; bottom: MM; 96: The Eaton Collection/AO/F22G-1-0-23; 97, top: Jessop/NAC/PA-30212; bottom: Muriel Wood; 98, top: NAC/C-9480; bottom: NPA/MM/1027, view; 99: NAC/PA-41785; 100: Archives, The Hospital for Sick Children; 101: John Boyd/NAC/PA-60732; 103: CTA/#1797; 105: AO/S-1243; 106: National Aviation Museum, Ottawa; 107: NAC/PA-110154.

Index

Page numbers in italics refer to illustrations, paintings, or photographs.